Tawheed al Mufaddal

Conversation between Imam Jafar Sadiq (asws)
and
His Faithful Companion

Mufaddal ibn Umar

Translated
by
Syed Jazib Reza Kazmi

Wilayat Mission Publications

Copyright © 2014 Syed Jazib Reza Kazmi
Cover Art Copyright © Shia Graphics
(http://www.facebook.com/shiagraphics)

Published by Wilayat Mission Publications®
Web: http://www.wilayatmission.org
Email: publications@wilayatmission.org

Second Edition 2014

All rights reserved. No part of this publication may be reproduced, stored in a retrieval system, or transmitted in any form or by any means, electronic, mechanical, photocopying, or otherwise without the prior written permission of the copyright holder.

First Printed 2012

All rights reserved.

ISBN-13: 978-0615947037
ISBN-10: 0615947034

DEDICATION

We present this meager offering before Imam e Zamana (atfs) without His help and blessings we would not have been able to complete. It is a great honor and blessing for us to be able to share with all momineen such glorious teachings of Masoomeen (asws).

We pray our offering is accepted and that we move one step closer to fulfilling the oath that we promised to fulfill.

TABLE OF CONTENTS

CHAPTER ONE: BACKGROUND 1

CHAPTER TWO: SESSION 5

THE HUMAN BEING 7
CREATION OF MAN 10
TEETH AND BEARD 11
ABSURDITY OF ATHEISM 13
TEARS 15
SALIVA 15
SEXUAL ORGANS 16
GENERAL ORGANS 16
NUTRITION 18
GENERAL DEVELOPMENT OF THE HUMAN BODY 19
EXCELLENCE OF MAN OVER ANIMALS 20
THE FIVE SENSES 20
SYSTEMS IN PAIRS AND SINGLE UNITS 23
VOICE 24
TONGUE AND LIPS 25
PROTECTIVE SYSTEM 25
HAIR AND NAILS 30
SALIVA 32
COVERING OF THE STOMACH 33
URGES 34
PHYSICAL FACULTIES 35
PSYCHOLOGICAL FACULTIES 37
SPEECH AND WRITING 38

RESTRICTION OF KNOWLEDGE 40
DREAMS 43
CATERING FOR HUMAN NEEDS 44
DISTINCTIVE FEATURES 46
LIMITED GROWTH 47
FATIGUE AND PAIN 47

CHAPTER THREE: SECOND SESSION 51

ANIMAL KINGDOM 53
ANIMAL WORLD 54
ELEPHANT 60
GIRAFFE 61
MONKEY 62
ANIMAL SKIN 63
BURYING THE DEAD 63
ANIMAL INSTINCT 64
PYTHON AND THE CLOUD 65
ANT 66
SPIDER 67
BIRD 68
HEN 69
BIRD'S CROP 70
BIRD'S FEATHERS 70
LONG-LEGGED BIRDS 71
PROVISION OF FOOD 71
NIGHT BIRDS 72
BEE 74
LOCUSTS 75
FISH 75

CHAPTER 4 THIRD SESSION 79

- ENVIRONMENT 81
- SKY 82
- SUNRISE AND SUNSET 82
- FOUR SEASONS 83
- SUN 84
- MOON 85
- STARS 86
- UNIVERSE 90
- DAYS AND NIGHTS 91
- HEAT AND COLD 92
- EARTH 95
- AIR 97
- FIRE 97
- WATER 98
- RAIN 100
- MOUNTAINS 102
- VEGETATION 104
- GRAINS 104
- PROPAGATION OF PLANTS 106
- LEAVES 107
- SEEDS 108
- POMEGRANATE 109
- CREEPER PLANTS 109
- DATE PALM 110
- WOOD 111
- HERBS 111
- WORTHLESS THINGS 112

CHAPTER FIVE: FOURTH SESSION 115

NATURAL DIASTERS 117
TROUBLE FREE LIFE 119
DEATH 124
CRITICIZING THE DIVINE ORDINANCE 125
REASON AND THE CREATOR 129

Chapter One

BACKGROUND

In The Name of Allah, The Beneficent The Merciful

Muhammad Ibn Sanan relates that Mufaddal Ibn Umar narrated the following to him:

One day after the Asr prayers, I sat between the mimbar and the shrine of the Holy Prophet (s.a.w.), contemplating on the exalted attributes which had been bestowed upon our Master, Syed Muhammad Mustafa (saw). Many of which the general Ummah paid little to no attention to nor did they have full understanding of the greatness of His eminence, perfect merifs, and His outstanding grandeur.

While I was immersed in such thoughts, Ibn Abi Al Auja, an atheistic pagan arrived there and took his seat within my hearing distance. A comrade of his followed him and sat listening to him.

Ibn Ali Auja started the conversation with the remark, "The occupant of this shrine has attained a unique station regarding His status and elevated honour." His comrade, adding an affirmation said: "He was a philosopher and made a mighty claim supported by miracles that confounded common sense. The learned intellects attempted to explain the mysteries in their depth but were unable to do so. When his mission became accepted by the sophisticated and the learned, then the common people entered into the fold of his faith one by one. All the places of worship and the mosques wherever the call to his prophethood reached, began to ring loud and clear with his name along with that of the Almighty Allah, regardless of where they were located. Not just once but five times a day whenever the Adhan and Iqamah were recited. He got his name attached to that of Allah (swt) in order to obtain popularity and notoriety and to keep His mission alive amongst the people."

Ibn Ali Auja remarked, "Leave aside the mention of Muhammad (saw) for I'm unable to comprehend Him in His reality. Instead let us talk about the basis of the people's acceptance of the faith of Muhammad (saw), the belief in the Sustainer of the universe. Does such a Creator exist or not?"

Then he referred to the origin and creation of the vast universe. He made the preposterous claim that no one had created them and there exists no Creator, nor Designer, nor Renovator. The universe came into being by itself and will continue to exist as such for all of eternity.

I was outraged to hear this and said to him, "O disbeliever! Do you disbelieve in the faith of Allah (swt) by totally denying the existence of Him, who created you, transforming you from one state to another, till you arrived at your present form? Had you looked at your own self and contemplated how you came into existence then you would have recognized within your own self obvious proofs of the existence of the Almighty Allah."

He said: "If you can provide well founded proofs, then we shall discuss this issue with you, and will admit to your being correct. However if you unable to provide such proofs, then you should not speak until you are able to do so especially if you are from the companions of Imam Jafar (asws) ibn Muhammad (saw). It is not His way of addressing issues and therefore you should follow His example and not speak in such an ill manner. He has listened to our discussions more than you have and has never spoken to us in the manner which you have. He acts with dignity, respect, and intelligence. He is never harsh or rude. He listens to our arguments with attentiveness and invites us to discuss matters with Him. Whenever we think we have finally outwitted Him and silenced Him, with just a few words, He is able to resume the debate and defeats even the most knowledgeable of us. We are left unable to reply to His proofs. If you are of His companions, then speak to us in the same manner as He does."

After hearing their words, I came out of the shrine dejected and thoughtful due to their disbelief in the existence of a Creator and due to their words towards me. I immediately went to my master, Imam Jafar Al Sadiq (asws). Upon seeing me, He asked me the reason for my looking so saddened and dejected. I related to Him the conversation of those atheists and the way I had tried to refute their arguments.

He told me to come the next day when he would explain to me how the Almighty Allah manifests His immense brilliance through the comprising of the universe, the animals, the birds, the insects, all living beings, those in the both the animal and vegetable kingdoms, through the trees whether they bear fruit or not and those which are edible as well as those which are not. Such descriptions of brilliance would be absolute proof against the disbelievers and a source of solace for the believers while at the same time silencing the pagans.

Chapter Two

SESSION

THE HUMAN BEING

At dawn I presented myself before my Master, and after gaining permission, I waited respectfully in the presence of my Master and upon being offered I took my seat. Then Imam (asws) retreated to the closet where He often went for solitude. I rose and waited for permission to follow Him. Upon being ordered to follow, I also rose up and entered the closet after Him. He sat and I sat before him.

He said, "Mufaddal! I feel you have had a troublesome night and are anxious about the events of tomorrow." I replied that I was.

He began, "Allah (swt) existed before there was anything and He will exist beyond eternity. May He be glorified in that He has made His revelation to us. To Him is due our deep gratitude because of His gift upon us. He bestowed glory upon Us through exalting Our knowledge and distinguished Us with the illustrious status of the progeny of Moula Ali (asws), and raised Us above the creation by entrusting Us with His hidden knowledge.

I requested permission to be able to write down all that He said to me, as I had the necessary writing material with me, to which Imam (asws) graciously agreed.

Then Imam (asws) said, "O Mufaddal! The disbelievers failed to grasp the mysteries and underlying causes of the origins of the creation, and they remain unaware of the faultless ingenuity that lies underneath the creation of the varied species of the sea and the land, the level and the rough.

They became disbelievers, and because of a deficiency of their knowledge and lack of intellect, began quibbling inimically with Haq (truth), so much so that they denied creativeness and claimed that all this universe was meaningless and vain, without any ingenious design on the part of a Designer or Creator - a purposeless non-entity without balance or reason.

Allah (swt) is far above what they attribute to Him. Misguided are they! In their misguidedness and bewilderment they are like the blind people groping right and left in a well-furnished, well-built house with fine carpets, luscious articles of food and drink, various kinds of clothing and other necessities of essential use, all adequately supplied in proper quantity and placed with perfect decorum and ingenious design. However, due to their blindness they fail to see the building and its furnishings. They move about from one room to ,another, advancing and retreating. If by chance, any one of them finds anything in its place to supply a need, and not knowing the purpose for which it is set there and unaware of the underlying brilliance, then he may begin to curse the architect of the building, but in reality, the fault lies within his own inability to see.

This analogy holds true in the case of the sect who deny the creative factor and the argument in favour of Divine Design. Failing to appreciate the merit of their provision, the perfection of creation and the beauty of design, they start wandering in the wide world, bewildered by their inability to understand the underlying causes and principles.

Even if one from amongst them is aware of the existence of a something, but is ignorant as to its true reality, purpose and need, then he immediately begins to find fault with it saying, "it is without doubt wrong".

The followers of Mani (the man who founded the Zoroastrianism sect in the time of King Shapur son of Urdsher, who believed in the prophethood of Isa (a.s.), but denied that of Musa (a.s.), and who believed in the duality of divinity as the creators of all good and evil in the universe - one light as the creator of all good things, the other darkness, as that of beasts and harmful creatures) have begun to openly to proclaim their heresies, and there are others besides them who are misguided and have also gone astray by declaring certain facts to be impossible or illogical.

It is incumbent upon the person whom Allah has endowed with the understanding of reality and whom He has guided to His faith and who has been granted insight in pondering upon the glorious design that underlies the creation and who is gifted with the reason and understanding to glorify Almighty Allah absolutely as his Lord for bestowing such favors upon him and to pray to Allah for an increase in understanding and a steadfastness therein.

Allah (swt) says,

"If you are grateful, I would certainly give to you more, and if you are ungrateful, My chastisement is truly severe (Sura Ibrahim ayah 7)"

The structure of the universe is the foremost direct proof of existence of Almighty Allah; the way the parts within have been joined together with elegant design. Upon reflection, one can easily understand this universe can be compared to a house that is furnished with all of the necessities human beings require.

The sky is like a canopy; the earth is spread out like a carpet, while the stars are set throughout the universe and appear as lamps alight in their places. The gems are treasured as if the house has lots of collections. Besides these, everything is readily available to meet individual needs. Man, in this world, is like the masterful owner of the house, having in his possession everything that is contained therein.

There also exists the different plant species. Some as fodder for the animals, others as medicines for human beings; some merely for decoration, while some supply fragrance; some as nutriment for man; some are for birds only and others for the beasts alone and so on. Different species of animals have been assigned different functions each to meet a specific requirement.

CREATION OF MAN

We shall start with a description of the creation of man as it is essential you learn its lessons before continuing on. The first step in the creation of man is when the embryo in the womb is adjusted even though it is confined within three distinct kinds of coverings and three kinds of darkness. The first covering is the outer wall. The second is the womb itself, and the third is the placenta. During this stage, the embryo can neither provide nourishment for itself nor keep harm away from itself.

Just as water carries nourishment to the plants, the menstrual flow is diverted to carry nourishment to the embryo. This process continues until the embryo passes onto the next stage of development where his skin becomes hardened enough to withstand the effects of the outside world on it and the eyes became able to withstand light. Once all of these processes are complete, the mother begins to feel the pains of labor which ends in the birth of the infant.

Once the infant has been born, the menstrual flow is again diverted. This time its taste and color are altered and it is redirected and becomes the milk which the mother shall provide as nourishment to the infant.

Instinctively at birth, the infant is able to indicate its need for milk and obtains his nourishment from the milk for as long as his body remains fragile and his organs soft and weak.

TEETH AND BEARD

As he grows and becomes in need of solid food in order for his body to grow stronger, his molars appear to aid in chewing the food to facilitate the digestive process.

As the male matures, hair begins to appear on his face as a sign of him having reached the age of manhood and exited his adolescence.

A female's face is hairless and clean. Thus preserving her attraction to the males and helping to continue the survival of the race.

Just imagine for a moment, that man passes through all of these different stages of perfection without having a Designer and a Creator? What would have happened to the embryo had the menstrual flow not been diverted for its nourishment? It would have dried up just as the plants do when deprived of water.

And if after the time for birth arrives were there no labor pains, would it not have become buried alive within the womb just as some are buried alive within the earth? Would it not have starved to death if suitable milk had not been supplied to it? If he were not fed the appropriate nourishment according to his developmental needs and if his teeth had not come at the appropriate time, would it not have been difficult for him to eat, chew and digest his food? If he remained as an infant dependent upon milk for nourishment and incapable of caring for himself or performing any work, would he not have been a burden upon his mother, keeping her busy looking after his needs and also keeping her from having the time for a second child if she desired?

Had hair not grown on his face at the proper time, then would he not have remained as an adolescent?

Who else then is it, Who created man from nothingness, and Who became the Architect of His Worth, Who is Ever-vigilant to supply his needs from time to time?

ABSURDITY OF ATHEISM

If abiogenesis (spontaneous creation without specific design) can be admitted under such conditions of regularity, then purposeful generation and definitely balanced creation can be the result of error and perplexity, since these two are opposed to abiogenesis.

It is absurd to say that order and integrity come about without a Creator, and disorder and impropriety of design and fate comes about with a Creator. He who says this is ignorant, because anything produced without design will never be exact and proportioned, while disorder and contradiction cannot be found within orderly design. Allah (swt) is far above what the heretics say.

If an infant were born with full intellect, then he would have been overwhelmed by the world around him. He would have felt lost in a strange world surrounded constantly by various different forms and animals.

It would be similar to a man who migrates to another country after being in prison for a time. If he has full intellect, then you will find him to be overwhelmed and lost for he will be unable to learn the new language and local customs quickly. Likewise if a person is taken prisoner to a foreign land at a young age, then you will see that he easily and quickly learns the local language and adapts more readily to the local customs.

Also if a child were born with a mature intellect, then he would feel shame and disgust at having to be cared for the way a mother cares for her child, feeding, clothing, and cleaning him.

If a child were born with mature intellect, it would also cause the adults in charge of their care to not have the same feelings of fondness and concern for the child as they do a child born without a mature intellect. This is why a child is born into this world while being completely unaware of the world and what lies therein. He sees the world through his limited understanding and therefore does not become overwhelmed by it.

His intellect and understanding increases little by little so as to gradually introduce him to his surroundings and accustomed his brain without enticing his curiosity and causing him to be overwhelmed and confused. This enables him to receive his sustenance with content and allows him to learn life's lessons of obedience and disobedience through trial and error.

There are other aspects as well which are the reason behind an infant being born with inferior intellect. The main reason being the love and affection which is felt by the parents for their offspring would not exist especially considering the difficulties parents face when raising and caring for their children. A child born with mature intellect would also not be in need of its parents care and the bond which develops between child and parent would not exist. In such circumstances, even a mother or a sister would have become like strangers to him and as such within wedlock limits.

Don't you see that everything big or small has been created on a flawless plan without fault or error?

TEARS

Just look at the advantages that occur due to a child's crying. There is a fluid in the child's brain which, if not drained off, may cause trouble or illness, even the loss of an eye. The discharge of the fluid from its brain leaves it healthy and the eyes brighter. The child is benefited by weeping, while his parents in their ignorance, try to prevent his weeping by catering for his wishes, not knowing the benefits thereof.

There are similar other advantages which the atheists fail to grasp and if they could have grasped them, they would not have denied the existence of such benefits therein. The gnostics (arifs) understand what the deniers do not. It occurs upon occasion that the creation do not understand the wisdom behind a particular happening. However the Creator is aware of the knowledge hidden within.

SALIVA

If the saliva is not allowed to flow from the mouths of children, then it can cause serious illnesses and derangements of the child. Almighty Allah has ordained that this fluid should be discharged by way of the mouth to keep him healthy in later age.

The Divine Creator has granted this blessing and they are ignorant of its benefits and the wisdom contained therein. They have been allowed this time in order to gain the wisdom of such benefits. Had these people appreciated all of these blessings then they would not have remained in sin for so long. So all praise and Glory is due to Him. How

Grand is His Beneficence. His blessings are for all whether deserving or undeserving. He is far exalted above what these misguided persons say.

SEXUAL ORGANS

Just consider the male and female organs of copulation. The male organ is capable of stimulation and increases in order to spawn the uterus with sperm. The male organ by itself is incapable of developing the fetus and as such requires the transfer of the sperm to the uterus of the female. The uterus serves as a deep receptacle fit to preserve efficiently the two seminal fluids, to develop the fetus by expanding proportionately , to prevent any pressure on it, to preserve it till it is strengthened and is toughened. Is it not so designed by a All Seeing Designer? Have all these works of ingenuity, or these elegant proportions come about by themselves? Allah Almighty is far exalted above the blasphemy of the polytheists.

GENERAL ORGANS

Just consider the various organs of the body, the functions each one is required to perform and the perfection of design that underlines each of them.

Both hands are meant to handle business, both feet are meant for locomotion, the eyes are to see with, the mouth is to take in food, the stomach is to digest it, the liver is to extract its nutrition for distribution to the various parts of the body after manufacturing the same into blood, bile, lymph and phlegm, the orifices of the body are meant to eliminate waste products. You shall find every organ exactly fitted to perform its specific functions and is created with perfect design."

I said, "Master! Some people believe that all this is the outcome of the function of nature - each organ coming into existence as and when required by nature."

Imam (asws) said: "Just ask them "Does the nature that functions in such a well-planned and well-ordered fashion possess knowledge and power or is it devoid of intelligence and reason, without power and without knowledge?" If they admit that it possesses knowledge and power, then what stops them from having a belief in the Creator? We say "All things are created by One Who is Master of Knowledge and Power". They say that there is no Creator but they admit that nature had done this with ingenuity and plan. As such nature is the cause of their creation, while they deny the Creator.

If they say that nature produces such things without knowledge (not knowing what it is doing) and without having the power to do it, but also is flawless in its design and built upon logic and reason, then this type of thinking is illogical and unacceptable. It is obvious that the outcome comes from an All Knowing Creator who has created a process and laid it down amongst the creation and it is that process that they call as "nature" when in reality it is the plan of an All Knowing Creator. In other words, Almighty Allah has ordained a method to produce everything according to its definite cause and principle.

As for instance, a seed needs water to sprout - no rain no corn; a child is born by the union of man and woman, and without this procedure of union and insemination, no child can be born: water evaporates to cause a cloud, the cloud is moved about by air to give rain; there can be no rain without such a process.

These atheists took at these causes and nature as the real Creator, denying the existence of the Creator above all these. This is manifest error, seeing that water is lifeless, and unless it is enlivened by the Life-giver, how can it produce corn? And how can the sperm which is without intelligence, develop into an infant, unless energized by the All Aware and All Knowing to create a head out of one part, hands and feet from other parts, bones from yet another part and heart and liver from another? Other forms of creation can be considered accordingly.

NUTRITION

Just consider the nutrition supplied to the body, and the brilliant plan underlying it. Just note that on the arrival in the stomach, the food is processed into chyme of the physicians and the extract is transferred to the liver by fine capillaries forming a network in that organ. The stomach is a rectifier for transfer of material to the liver in rectified form, in order to prevent injury to that delicate structure.

The liver then takes up the extract of the nutriment, and by an unexplainable brilliance, changes it into blood to be pumped by the heart to all parts of the body by means of blood vessels, the same can be seen in the irrigation channels of gardens and fields supplying water to any place required to be irrigated. All waste products and toxic wastes are carried off to organs designed to eliminate them, e.g. the gall bladder, the intestines, sweat glands of the armpits and thighs etc. The bile matter goes to the gall bladder, some matter goes to the spleen and the moisture goes to the bladder.

Just consider the ingenuity that has gone into the building up of the body! How well are these organs co-ordinated! How the vessels, the intestines and the bladder etc. are organized to collect the waste products of the body so as to prevent them from being scattered all over the body to cause disease and weakness.

Glory be then to Him Who created these organs according to a remarkable plan and design. All Praise is due to Him, Who is worthy of it".

GENERAL DEVELOPMENT OF THE HUMAN BODY

I said: "Please master! Explain to me the gradual development of the body stage by stage."

Imam (asws) said, "The first stage of this development is the embryo in the womb - invisible to the eye and inaccessible to the hand. Its development proceeds till he is perfected in body with all organs and parts complete in every detail, the heart, the liver, the intestines and all working parts, the bones, muscles, fat, the brain, tendons, blood-vessels, the cartilages etc. are all fully developed.

He enters this world, and you see how his intellect as well his physical body continues to develop, preserving at the same time all his features without any addition or reduction. The body progresses on while retaining its well-knit form, till its maturation, regardless if its life span is lengthy or short. Is not his profound planning and brilliance elegantly designed by the All Knowing designer?

EXCELLENCE OF MAN OVER ANIMALS

Just consider the excellence of man's creation over the animals. He stands erect and sits squarely to enable him to hold things in his hands, to acquire them with his organs, to work, to plan. If man walked on all fours like animals, he would not have been able to perform the tasks he does now.

THE FIVE SENSES

The five senses are specifically superior to those of animals in point of constitution and efficiency so as to endow wih him special merit.

The eyes are set in the head as if a lamp set on a lamp post to enable him to see everything. They are not set in the lower parts of the feet to safeguard against injuries or accidents during work or movement, which would have ailed them and impaired their efficiency. Had they been set in the middle part of the body like the belly, the back or the breast etc., it would have been difficult to revolve them or to see things by sudden turning. The head is the best suitable place for these senses in comparison with any other organ.

The senses are five in number to respond to all kinds of stimuli and to leave no stimulus undetected.

The eyes distinguish between colours. The colours would have been meaningless without a means of recognition, especially since these colours exist as a means to distinguish one thing from one another.

The ears are set in the head to detect sounds. Again these sounds would have been meaningless had there not been a way for them to be heard. Similar is the case with other senses—without the sense of taste, all tasteful foods would have been dull; without the sense of touch the sensation of heat, cold, softness, hardness, would just as well have been non-existent; and without the sense of smell, all scents would have been lifeless.

Likewise, if there had been no colours, then the eyes would have had no purpose. Without sound, the ears may as well be nonexistent. So just consider how it has been ordained that there is a definite correspondence between the sense organ and the sensation it is connected with. We cannot hear with our eyes, nor distinguish colours with our ears, nor smell except through our nose, and so on.

Then there are other variables between the sense organ and the sensation stimulus, without which the link cannot be established. As for example, in the absence of light to reflect colour, the eyes fail to recognize colour, and without air to set up sound waves, the ears would not be able to detect any sound.

Can it be then hidden, from one who has been endowed with sound reason and one who utilizes his intellect correctly, after all the details I have given about the inter-connection between the sense organs, the sensation stimulus, and the related variables linking them to complete the process, that all this has been planned and executed by the All Knowing Almighty Allah.

Can such harmony, such brilliance come about spontaneously? How can nature by itself perceive how the eye or the ear is to be constructed, and what functions each is to perform and what medium is to suit each as a means for correct comprehension in order to create each? Is it conceivable for an unaware, unknowing nature is capable of such planning, unless the Almighty Designer plans them on the basis of perfect understanding?

Just consider the case of a person who has lost his eyesight and the loss he suffers in his day-to-day working. He cannot see where he is going, whether his feet fall in a hole or go uphill, nor can he see ahead, nor can he recognize colours, nor can he appreciate a pleasing or a forbidden face. He will not be able to know hollow ground, nor know an enemy with a drawn sword, nor can he undertake any of the handicrafts like writing, business or trinket-making. His brain does suggest certain ways to enable him to move about or take his food, without which he would be little better than a stone at rest.

Similar is the case of a man deficient in hearing. He suffers loss on many counts. He has no relish for conversational talk nor a sense for pleasant or unpleasant sounds. People have difficulty in conversing with him, he gets annoyed with his self. Though alive, he is like a dead man in respect of talking. Though present, yet he is like a man far away unaware of any news about.

The person devoid of intelligence is worse than cattle, because even the cattle are able to recognize and understand things which he is unable to. Do you not think that these organs, systems, intellect and everything else required for his orientation (without which the perfection of his design is imperfect) are duly provided? Have all these been produced without balance, power and knowledge? Certainly not! They are necessarily the outcome of definite Design and Planning of the Almighty Designer". I asked, "Master! How is it that some people are lacking in those organs and systems, and undergo the losses that you have described?"

Imam (asws) said, "It is for the warning of the person lacking them and other people as well. The monarch warns his subjects in such ways and such warning is hardly resented, rather it is appreciated advice.

The people who are thus afflicted will be recompensed after death, provided they are grateful to Allah (swt) and turn to Him, so munificently that all the troubles undergone by them due to lack of such organs, will appear trivial in comparison. So much so that if after death they are allowed the choice to return to those troubled, they would welcome the opportunity to earn higher recompense.

SYSTEMS IN PAIRS AND SINGLE UNITS

Just consider the wisdom and balanced design underlying the production of organs and systems in pairs or as single units. Just consider the head which is created a single unit and the appropriateness of it being created as a single unit. A second head would have been only an additional weight, quite unnecessary, seeing that one piece comprises all the senses needed for man. Two heads would have meant two parts for men. So, if he used only one for talk, the other would have been redundant. To have used both simultaneously for the same talk would have been meaningless.

A person would have been limited in his ability to work and perform tasks if he had been created with only one hand instead of two. Don't you see that a carpenter or a mason would be unable to carry on his profession if one of his hands gets paralyzed? And in case he tries to do his work with a single hand, he cannot perform it as dexterously and efficiently as with the help of both hands.

VOICE

Just consider a man's voice and conversation, and the make up of the organs necessary for speech. The larynx, which produces the sound, is like a tube while the tongue, the lips and the teeth mould the sound into letters and words.

Don't you see that a person who loses his teeth cannot reproduce the sound of the letter 's'; he who gets his lips cut cannot pronounce 'f', while a thick tongue cannot give the sound of 'r'? A bagpipe resembles it a great deal. The larynx is comparable to the pipe and the bag into which air is blown, corresponds to the lungs containing air. The muscles controlling the lungs to produce sounds resemble the fingers pressing; the air of the bag into the pipe. The lips and the teeth which mould the sounds into letters and words correspond to the fingers on the orifices of the pipe giving rise to music and song. The larynx here has been regarded as an analogue to the bagpipe by way of explanation, whereas in reality the bagpipe is the instrument constructed on the pattern of the natural organ, the larynx.

The organs of speech mentioned here are sufficient for a correct pronunciation of the letters. There are, however, other functions associated to these. The larynx, for instance, is so fashioned as to admit fresh air into the lungs for supply to the blood and heart, which if it fails even for a moment, would result in death.

TONGUE AND LIPS

The tongue is designed in such a way as to be able to decipher the different tastes of the foods such as the sweet from the sour and the salty from the sweet. The tongue also helps to feel the pleasantness of water and food. The teeth chew the food to make it soft enough for easy digestion. They also hinder the lips from being sucked into the mouth. A person who has lost his teeth is seen to have loosely moving lips. The lips help to suck in water, so as to allow only a specified amount of water to enter the stomach as required, instead of flooding down of its own accord and producing suffocation in the throat, or leaving to some sort of internal inflammation by virtue of its forceful flow. Moreover, the two lips serve as a door to keep the mouth shut at will.

We have explained to you the diverse functions performed by them and the benefits coming from them, as well as how the same organ may serve different purposes.

PROTECTIVE SYSTEM

If you look at the brain, you will find it wrapped up in membranes one upon the other to protect it from injuries and movement. The skull protects it as a helmet against being shattered to pieces by a knock or blow upon the head. The skull is covered with hair like a fleecy covering, safeguarding it against heat and cold.

Who, then, except Almighty Allah endowed the brain with such security and protection, and Who made it the principal source of sense perception, and Who made the arrangements for its extra-ordinary protection in comparison with all other parts of the body because of its important status in the body?

Just consider the eye-lid, how it is fashioned as a screen for the eye with the eye-lashes like the strings, for raising and lowering the screen. Just notice how the eye-ball is set in a cavity shaded by the screen and hair. Who has concealed the heart within the breast and covered it with a screen which you call the membrane? Who has arranged for its protection by means of the ribs, the muscles and flesh interwoven in such a way as to prevent anything getting to it to cause an abrasion? Who has shaped the two holes in the throat - one for its production of the sound connected with the lungs and the other called the gullet leading to the stomach for entry of the food. And who has placed a flap, the epiglottis, over the hole leading to the larynx, to prevent food entering the lungs, which would cause death if not thus managed? Who has caused the lungs to fan air to the heart arduously without rest to remove the toxins that would destroy it otherwise?

Who has shaped the sphincters, controlling the outlets of urine and stool, like the strings of a purse, to be opened or shut at will and not be dripping all the time, automatically resulting in a persistent nuisance in life? Similarly there are matters which a computer may compute, but others which men have no knowledge of and are beyond computation.

Who has given such resilience to the muscles of the stomach that it has been commissioned to digest coarse foods? And who has made the liver soft and tender to accept nutriment in purified and rectified form and function more finely than the stomach? Can all these tasks be completed by anyone except the All Powerful, All mighty? Can you imagine that all this can be performed by lifeless nature? Certainly not! All this is the planning of the Almighty All Powerful Designer, Who has the fullest knowledge supreme over the creation. He is Allah, the All-knowing, Almighty.

Just consider why the tender marrow is kept protected inside bone tubes - just for the sake of protecting it against waste under the influence of the sun's heat which might melt it, or that of cold which might solidify it, which would end life—the bone marrow being an essential ingredient supplying the body's needs for energy.

And why is this circulation of blood confined in the blood vessels, except that it should function in the body and not flow off? Why are these nails fixed on fingers, except that they afford protection against damage and help in better efficiency, for without them the presence of flesh alone would not have enabled man to pick up things with a pinch, to use a pen for writing or to thread a needle?

Why is the ear patterned intricately as a prison-house, except that the sounds may be carried to the membrane for detection without damage thereto by the violence of air impact?

Why is this flesh woven over man's thighs and buttocks, other than to bring him comfort when sitting upon the hard floor?

Who has created the human race as man and woman? It is he Who ordained the race to flourish by the method of the union of the two sexes or at least to maintain its numerical strength, through the differentiation of the two sexes.

And who made him the forefather of a generation? Surely it was He Who implanted hope in him. Had not this desire been implanted within his heart, then he would not have had this desire to mutual union. Look at the living beings reproduction among whom it is not conditioned by union and sexuality, but is effected by a certain stage of development of the female. They have no differentiations of male and female at all. Can anyone, for instance, tell between the female and male of a wasp?

And who gave him organs for action? And who made him a worker? Surely He Who created him needy, for man would not have worked if he had no need to fulfill. If he did not need to satisfy his hunger, why should he have laboured, why should he have taken to business and industry? Had he no need to safeguard his body against heat and cold, why should he have learnt sewing, needle manufacture, spinning, weaving, cotton growing etc. And in the absence of all this, of what use would have been the organs of action and the fingers? And who created him needy? And who created for him the factors of neediness? Surely He Who took upon Himself the responsibility for supplying the needs

Who endowed him with intellect? Surely He Who made reward and chastisement as essential for him. He would not need intellect if he were not responsible for reward and punishment. The Almighty Creator endowed him with intellect to distinguish between good and evil, having decided upon reward and punishment as essential to him - to get the reward for goodness and chastisement for evil. The animate beings which are not subject to reward and punishment have no sense of good and evil, nor do they know the distinction between the haram (forbidden) and the halal (lawful), the condemned and the approved types of action. They recognize, however, the factors needed by them for survival of their species or individuality. As for instance, the bird has the necessary recognition of an eagle as a bird of prey, and so at its very sight takes to speedy flight; the deer knows well that the lion would tear him up, so at its mere sight, it flees for life.

Who has endowed him with strategy and discernment? Surely He Who has gifted him with energy. And who has gifted him with energy? Surely He Who has ordained justification of conduct on him. Who helps him in all these undertakings, in which his plans fail? Surely He Who deserves our highest gratitude.

Just consider what I have explained to you. Can there be such orderliness and method in the absence of planning? Certainly not! Allah Almighty is far exalted above what these people say.

Supposing you found one shutter of a door having a latch fixed to it. Can you imagine it to have been fixed without any purpose? Surely you will conclude that it is there to be joined to the other shutter for a definite advantage. Similarly you will find a male creature as one individual of a pair created for the female individual for union to preserve the race.

May Allah (swt) destroy those who claim to be philosophers, but are so blind in their approach to such wonders of creation and constitution that they deny in the creation of the universe the design of the Almighty Designer and the Will of the Master Planner.

Just look with respective eyes at the great benefits of Allah, the Almighty, in the relief of trouble after taking in food and drink. Is it not an elegance of plan in the construction of a house that the lavatory should be in a secluded part thereof? In the same way, Allah the Almighty has made the orifice for the excreta of man in a secret place. It is not in the open nor has it prominence, but is so situated as to be perfectly hidden. When a man needs to answer the call of nature and assumes the requisite posture of sitting, the orifice allows the excreta to escape.

Just consider the teeth set in the mouth of man. Some are sharp, which incise and tear the food. Others are flat which chew and pulverize. Since both types are required, he is supplied accordingly.

HAIR AND NAILS

Just consider and appreciate the wisdom underlying why it is proper to have the hair cut and the nails trimmed. They grow and increase and so need to be clipped. As such they are devoid of sensation to avoid pain to man. If the clipping resulted in pain, then they would either have been left to grow indefinitely and become burdensome, or pain would have been inflicted in clipping."

I asked, "Master! Why were they not so designed as not to thrive to an extent that their clipping would be necessary?"

Imam (asws) said, "There are countless benefits of Allah the Almighty has bestowed upon His creatures unbeknownst to them, and if they knew, they would be grateful for.

Know that the troubles and ailments of the body are relieved through these hairs coming out of the pores. The fingers get relief of their ailments through the nails. That is why a weekly clipping of nails, shaving of head and removing of redundant hair must be effected, so that the nails and hairs should grow fast and relieve ailments and troubles. Ailments remain confided in the body otherwise with consequent pains and diseases.

No hair growth is allowed on parts of the body where they would harm man. If hair had grown inside the eyes, he would have been blinded. If they had grown inside the mouth, would not water and food have been hindered? If they had grown on the palms of hands, would not the sense of touch have been impaired and would not the same have interfered in the proper discharge of many a task, and the recognition by proper touch. There is great underlying brilliance as to keeping certain spots of the body hairless. Could nature have the insight of such subtleties or can such well-designed plans be attributed to it? Woe unto these atheists and their ignorance. This affair of creation, and see how error and harm of the beasts and other animals, whose procreation depends upon copulation, are similarly instanced.

You see that their entire bodies are covered with hair, with the exception of the particular parts for the same reasons. So consider this affair of creation and see how error and harm of methods have been avoided while rectitude and benefit have been secured.

When these followers of Mani and those of their kind tried to challenge the belief in purposeful creation, they found fault with the growth of hair on the pubis and armpits. They failed to grasp that such growth was due to the moisture flowing to those parts. The hair grows there just as grass grows at a place where water collects. Don't you see how spots are prepared to collect waste products and hold them?

Yet another strategy underlying it, is that it provides a man with yet another distraction relating to his body, and he is kept busy with the cleanliness of his body and the removal of his hair, and thus prevented from perpetrating acts of greed, cruelty, conceit and impudence, for which he may not get the opportunity.

SALIVA

Just consider the saliva in the mouth and see the wisdom underlying it. It is so composed as to ensure constant flow to keep the throat and the palate moist, not to allow dryness therein that they may lead to death. Without it the food would not be chewed nor would it flow down. All this is obvious and supported by observation. And know that this fluid is derived from food and aids the action of the gall-bladder.

COVERING OF THE STOMACH

Some ignorant debaters and half-witted claimants to philosophy have, because of their deficient understanding and faulty knowledge, said, "It would have been better if the belly of man had been like a cloak to enable the physician to open it at will, observe its contents and poke his hand inside for medical treatment, and not as it is, walled in, mysteriously hidden from the reach of eyes and hands. The internal disorders can now only be gauged by delicate symptoms of the examination of the urine, pulse etc., which are not above error ant doubt to the extent that such error in pulse and urine examination may lead to death."

Would that these ignorant claimants to philosophy and argument had known, that it would have removed all apprehension of disease and death. Man would have been infatuated with his immortality and healthfulness, which would have rendered him willful and conceited. The open belly would have allowed the constant trickling of moisture, thus spoiling his seat, bed and nice dresses; in short, his whole living would have been burdened under the circumstances.

The stomach, the liver and the heart function properly because of vital heat, which would have been disturbed by the influence of the outside air acting through the belly under treatment, open to the reach of the eye and the hand. This would have resulted in death.

Don't you see that all hypothesis of the real nature of creation and constitution are far-fetched and preposterous?

URGES

Just consider the matter of feeding, resting and sex, which are ordained for him and the expediencies underlying them. Each of them is propelled by an urge, which give rise to a desire and an excitation therefore. Hunger demands food which supplies life and energy to the body and its substance. Sleep demands rest for the recuperation of the body to remove the fatigue.

If man were to take food just for the needs of his body without an urge from within forcing him to feed, it is possible that he might have given way to laziness because of lethargy or pressure, his body would have been emaciated leading to death, just as a man puts off taking medicine which he only needs to improve his health. And this may have caused his death.

Similarly he may put off sleep out of procrastination and thereby weaken his body. If procreation were the sole aim of sexual union, it would not have been improbable on his part to slacken, with resulting decrease in population and final extinction, for there are people who have no desire for progeny nor any need therefore.

Behold, then, that very act concerning man's health and improvement has been reinforced by an insistent urge embedded in his nature prompting him thereto.

PHYSICAL FACULTIES

And know that the physical body has four faculties :

The affinitive faculty—This accepts the food and pushes it into the stomach.

The retentive faculty—This retains food for the natural processes to act thereon.

The assimilative faculty—This processes food to take out its nutrients for distribution to the body.

The eliminative faculty—This eliminates the waste products after the assimilative faculty has completed its function.

Just consider the adjustment made in the body amongst these facilities. These have been organized to meet the bodily needs as part of the All Knowing Design.

Without the affinitive faculty, how would he have exerted after cod, which is necessary for the upkeep and maintenance of its body?

Without the retentive faculty, how could the food have been retained in the stomach to be digested?

Without the assimilative faculty, how could the food have been processed to get the extract for supply to the body without disturbance?

And without the eliminative faculty, how could the waste products, given off by the stomach, have been eliminated regularly?

Don't you see how the Glorious Almighty Allah as ordained and appointed the faculties for the functions conditioning the Health of the body by His Consummate Skill and Supreme Will?

Let us illustrate it by an example. Just imagine the body to be a royal palace, with his servants and dependents residing herein. There are employees engaged in its management. One of them is entrusted with the task of supplying the provisions to the dependents. The second is charged with the task of storing the same, so that it may be kept for conversion into nutrition. The third has to process it and distribute it. The fourth sweeps the waste products left over.

The monarch of the palace is the All Knowing Creator Almighty, the Lord of the entire universe. The palace is man's body; the dependents are the organs of the body, while the four facilities are employees.

You may, perhaps, consider the explanation given by me concerning the four faculties and their functions as redundant and unnecessary. Yet my explanation does not follow the pattern of the books given by physicians, nor does the tenor of my talk follow theirs. Those people have made mention of the four faculties on the ground that it is needed in the medical art for healing. We mention it from the viewpoint of its need for invigorating the faith and reformation of the contrary minds, just like my comprehensive explanation illustrating the All Knowing Design.

PSYCHOLOGICAL FACULTIES

Reflect over the faculties embedded in the human psyche and the way they are organized, deliberation, superstition, reason, memory etc. What would be a man's plight if he were deprived of the faculty of memory, and how much would his life's affairs be disrupted. He would not have remembered what other people owe him and what he owes to others, what bargains he made, what he heard and what he said. He would not have remembered who did him a good turn and who an evil one, what profited him and what harmed him. He would not have remembered the path he traveled countless times. He would not have remembered anything even if he continued to learn a science all his life, nor would he have determined upon a belief or faith, nor could he have compared one thing with another by analogy. In fact, he would have been outside of humanity altogether. Just see how profitable to man are these faculties. Leave the others aside for now and just deliberate upon this one for now and the place it occupies within the daily life.

A benefit that is even greater than memory is forgetfulness. Without it, man would never find peace in any affliction, nor would he ever be free from frustration or hate. He would be unable to enjoy any of the benefits he finds in this world because of the constant memories of affliction, nor would he be able to rid himself of the feelings of envy that consume him. Don't you see how the opposite faculties of memory and forgetfulness have been created in man, each ordained with a definite purpose?

The benefits that arise from the combination of these two opposite faculties is a proof that they come from One

Creator and it is these seemless benefits that keep those who believe in two opposite creators of all the universe such as the followers of Mani from being able to give credit to their so called creators.

And those people, for instance the followers of Mani who believe in two opposite creators of all the universe, cannot give the credit forthe creation of these two opposite faculities to their so called opposite in any case be expected to regard those two opposite entities as the creators of these two opposite faculties, for these two faculties possess the benefits which you see accruing from them.

Just consider the quality with which man alone is endowed and no other creature shares it with him - modesty. Without it, no one would have shown hospitality to a guest, nor would anyone have fulfilled his promise or the needs of another nor any goodness would have been achieved. There are many obligations which are performed merely through modesty. The one who abandons modesty ignores the rights of his parents and his obligations within the family relation nor does he honor his oaths. Don't you see how all these qualities have been endowed in man so as to benefit him and help him in accomplishing his affairs?

SPEECH AND WRITING

Consider the blessing of speech bestowed upon man by Allah through which he is able to express his inner thoughts and feelings and through which he is able to understand the thoughts and emotions of others. Without this faculty he would have been like a wild beast who is unable to convey his own inner thoughts and also unable to understand the words of the one who is speaking.

The same applies to the art of writing which is a means for learning about the histories of people of long ago as well as a means of communication for existing generations to those who will come later. Also the achievements of science and literature can be preserved for countless generations to learn from and enjoy. Through writing man is also capable of preserving discussions that he has with others. Without this art, one era would be completely cut off from another and people would be unable to receive news from their native lands.

Sciences too would have become extinct. Information on morality and etiquette would have been lost and the affairs of mankind would have been damaged beyond repair because the religious teachings and traditions as well as the knowledge that man gains from reading such writings could not be passed from one era to the next.

You may, perhaps, think that this need has been fulfilled by man with the help of his own design and intelligence. However, these qualities are not inherent in the nature of man. The same is the case of speech and language. He who makes such a claim, the answer will be that though in both these matters man's planning and action have played a role, yet the means whereby his planning and action achieve the goal, is a gift from the bounty of Allah Almighty, underlying therein. If man had not been bestowed a tongue for speech or intellect to guide him in how to perform the action, then he would have never been able to speak. If he had not been blessed with palms and fingers, then it would have been impossible for him to write.

You should learn a lesson from the animals in this behalf, who have neither the power to speak nor the power to write. As such it is the principle laid down by the Almighty Creator for man's fundamental nature as a special blessing, for which whoever is grateful shall get the heavenly rewards, while whoever denies will be ignored, for Allah Almighty is independent of the whole universe.

RESTRICTION OF KNOWLEDGE

Contemplate on those matters which man has been given knowledge of as well as those matters he has not been given the knowledge of. The knowledge of Allah Almighty Creator is attainable through the proofs that are available within the creation as well as the knowledge pertaining to those matters which are obligatory upon him such as justice towards all human beings, kindness to parents, honouring oaths, sympathy towards the oppressed etc. This knowledge is possessed by all nations regardless if they are in agreement with Us or against Us.

Man has also been given the knowledge of those things which are beneficial to his worldly life, for example agriculture, horticulture, colonization, cattle farming, drawing water from the wells and the springs, herbal research for medical purposes, mining for different kinds of precious stones, diving in the sea, the different kinds of planning for hunting animals and birds, fishing, industry, trade and business methods and many other things. Such knowledge is made available to him as is in his best interests.

Matters that are beyond his comprehension and have no impact upon his position are not within his knowledge such as ilm ul ghayab (knowledge of the unseen), future or past events, what lies in the depths of the oceans or in the vast expanses of the universe, and what is within the minds and hearts of people.

Therefore man has only been given that knowledge which is essential for his worldly and religious affairs and has been prevented from knowing unnecessary things for his own benefit. Just think for a moment why has man not been given the knowledge of his own life span.

If he knew his life on earth to be short, then he would have spent his whole life being bitter and waiting for the moment of his death. He would be like one who has lost all of his possessions or one who is about to lose them. He would have felt impoverished and needy. How fearful would he be constantly expecting the destruction of his possessions and the resulting poverty that would come afterwards? The sorrow and remo the sorrow and frustration he would feel at the thought of death would be far greater than the thought of the destruction of his property because the one who loses his property always has the hope that one day he might get more in return and this hope would provide him with peace of mind.

The one who knew he had a long life span would be prone to extreme arrogance. He would become consumed with indecent and immoral activities believing that in his last days of life he would offer repentance for his present acts of immorality. Allah Almighty does not will such matters for His creation.

Imagine having a servant who disobeys you throughout the year in hopes that he will gain pardon after performing his duties for only a few days or month. Surely you would not like such a servant nor would you consider him to a righteous servant ever ready to do your bidding.

You might raise objection to this by saying "What about the man who is disobedient and then repents and his repentance is accepted?" Our answer to this is that this is only for that man who is obedient but at some point allows his nafs to overcome him. He is not one who is simply indulging in worldly passions for the moment while expecting forgiveness at a later stage.

The one who is willfully disobedient while expecting forgiveness at a later stage is attempting to deceive Allah, the One who cannot be deceived. He wishes to gain the pleasures of the moment while expecting to be forgiven due to his repentance later on, but he does not consider that due to his overindulgence of worldly pleasures that his physical body may become weakened and thereby prevent him from performing the necessary penances in his old age. It may also be that death would overcome him suddenly and also prevent him from being able to offer his repentance. He would be like the debtor who is able to repay his debts but procrastinates til death overtakes him. His blessings will be destroyed and his debts will testify against him. Therefore the knowledge of man's life span is kept secret from him so that he may expect death at any moment and under such circumstances would avoid transgressions and adopt righteous actions.

You may raise another objection that now that his life span is a secret from him and he is ever in suspense about his death, he commits evil deeds and unlawful acts. Our reply to this is that the Planning is in accordance with the situation prevailing now. If in spite of all this a man does not refrain from evil, it is a sign of his temperamental perversion and his hard heartedness. There is no error in the planning. If a patient, after being made fully aware of the benefits of certain medicines and the ill effects of certain behaviors, decides to ignore the directions of the physician, then it is not the physician that is to blame but the patient who decided to ignore the physician's orders. As such the suspense about death is better for him than his confidence in a long life.

While there is a category of people who, despite their suspense about death, are lazy and do not profit by advice, there is also another category who benefit from the advice, abstain from sinfulness and act righteously. They give to the needy and the indigent in charity of their nice possessions. It would not have been justice to deprive this category from getting the benefit thereof.

DREAMS

Just consider the dreams and the wisdom underlying them. There are dreams that come true and dreams that do not come true all mixed together. If all dreams are true, then all men would have been prophets. If all dreams were untrue, then they would have been useless, rather redundant and meaningless. The dreams that are sometimes true are those that benefit a person in his life's business, under their guidance, or to avoid the loss of and thus he has been informed thereby. Dreams are mostly untrue lest man may come to depend on them.

CATERING FOR HUMAN NEEDS

Just consider those things that are provided to meet human needs.

The earth to build houses, iron for industry, wood for building boats etc. Stone for use as grindstone, copper for utensils, gold and silver for business transaction, gems for treasure, corn for food, fragrant articles for pleasure, medicines to heal the sick, beasts of burden, dry wood as fuel, ashes for chemicals, sand for the benefit of the earth, is it possible for one to count the limitless bounties that are provided?

Do you think that if a man enters a house and sees it supplied with all human needs, the whole house is full of treasure and everything placed with a definite purpose, can he imagine all those things have been arranged by themselves without anyone to plan it? Then how can any rational being suggest that this world and all this contents have come by themselves?

Learn a lessons from the things that have been created to meet the needs of humans and the great ingenuity underlying them. Corn has been produced for him but he has been entrusted with the duty of grinding, kneading and cooking. Wool has been produced for him which he must gin, spin and weave. The tree is made for him but he must sow the seed, irrigate and supervise it. The herbs have been created as medicines for him but he must find them, mix them and compound them.

Similarly you will find all things made by the Creator to meet the needs of humans. No plan of man could work so sufficiently in their action and use thereof. The need and the situation for it has been left to him in his own interest. If Almighty Allah had created the provisions in such a way that man did not have to work to mold them to suit his needs, then man would have had nothing to do and would have become restless. He would have begun to walk about on the earth on all fours and the earth would not have been able to bear his burden. Man would not have had a happy life if all his needs had been fulfilled without effort and, nor would he have enjoyed such a thing.

Don't you see that a guest staying for a time with all his needs being fulfilled by the host steadily, without any effort on his part to secure eatables, drink, bedding or seating, gets tired of idleness and inactivity. He seeks some engagement. What would have been his condition if his inactivity were lifelong? This then is ordained for man to occupy his limits to transact his business in his own interests, lest idleness and inactivity cause him boredom. Moreover he should be prevented from such undertakings as are outside his capacity, and which have no advantage for him even if completed.

Know that a man's basic need is food and water. See the planning that has gone therein.

Man needs water more than bread, because he can bear hunger longer than thirst. He needs water for drinking, ablutions, washing clothes, watering animals, and irrigation of crops. Water, therefore, is provided in abundance without need to purchase it to save man the need for search. Bread must be obtained with effort and planning to keep man busy with his occupation and to hinder him from pride and conceit and useless undertakings.

Don't you see that a child in his early age is sent to a teacher for instruction to keep him away from playing away all his time, which may lead him or his kin to trouble. Similarly if man were left unoccupied, he would have taken to pride and conceit and would have indulged in actions likely to harm him grievously.

That men who are born into wealth and luxury and receives all of his needs from his kin is most likely to fall into such grievous conduct is a perfect illustration of this.

DISTINCTIVE FEATURES

Know why one man does not resemble another, like the birds and animals etc., having likened one with the other. You see a herd of deer and a swarm of partridges each resembling the other without much difference among them, whereas men, as you see, have distinctive features and constitutions, so much so, that no two men correspond to the same pattern.

The reason is that each individual of mankind needs to be recognized distinctly from the others based upon his physical appearance so that they can conduct business (which is not a a concern of the animals) amongst themselves. Don't you see that the mutual resemblance among animals and birds does them no harm? Not so in man, for if by chance a pair of twins become alike in shape, people feel a great deal of confusion in dealing with them. What must be given to one is handed to the other by mistake. One is held up in place of the other in retribution.

It so happens in other matters as well through resemblance. Human resemblance can be even more harmful.

Who then, has provided such niceties and perfections, which are beyond comprehension? Surely He Who created all these, Whose Grace extends to all things.

Will you believe a person who says that a picture on the wall, which you see, has come into being of itself without the aid of an artist? Certainly not! You will laugh at him. How then can you believe that a living man with faculties of speech and movement can come into being of himself, while you are not prepared to entertain such belief in regard to a lifeless picture?

LIMITED GROWTH

Why does it so happen that the bodies of men do not grow beyond a certain limit despite the fact they continue living and to feed? What is this due to if not to Profound Perception?

The Almighty Allah has so ordained that each species of living beings should have a definite limit of growth - no bigger nor smaller. They continue to increase up to that limit and then stop growing, even though they continue to feed. If it were not so ordained they would have continued to grow till their bodies would have grown out of recognizable limits.

FATIGUE AND PAIN

Why is it in the case of human beings in particular that movement and activity create fatigue in them and they avoid fine industries just because his needs like clothing etc., require more exertion? If man did not suffer hardness and pain, how could he have abstained from evil deeds, prostrated before Allah (swt) or sympathized with the people?

Don't you see that no sooner a man is inflicted with pain, than he turns in perfect humility towards Allah (s.w.t.), supplicating for restoration of his health before his Creator and opens his hands in munificence? If man had felt no pain in being beaten, how could the governments have reformed the dissidents? How could have children been taught sciences and arts? How could the slaves have been made to submit to their masters willingly?

Is there no admonition in all this for Ibn Abi Al Auja and his companions who deny Purpose, and the followers of Mani who deny the wisdom underlying labour and pain?

Supposing only males or only females had been created in living beings, would not their species have become extinct? It is thus to preserve their species, that a mixture of males and females is brought into being in the right proportion.

Why is it that when men and women reach puberty, the man alone grows a beard? Is it not in accordance with set Design? This is because the man is created as the maintainer over women. The woman is the supervisor of man's interests and his beloved. Man, as such, is bestowed with a beard to give him prestige and honourable appearance. The woman is allowed beauty and freshness instead as attractions for union.

Don't you see the flawless merits that this creation acquires by the Design of the Almighty Allah? Everything is according to a definite measure. Nothing is given which is not needed."

It was now afternoon, my Master rose for prayers telling me to come to him the next day, InshaAllah.

Overjoyed with the information received, I returned with a grateful heart for Allah (swt) for the blessing bestowed on me.

I had a very pleasant night due to the valuable instructions bestowed on me by my Master.

Chapter Three

SECOND SESSION

ANIMAL KINGDOM

At dawn I went to my Master (asws)'s house and upon obtaining His permission, I seated myself in His presence.

Imam (asws) began, "All Praise is due to Him Who is the Creator of revolution of the ages, Who brings one stage after another and one state after another of decades of time, to reward the righteous and to chastise the evil-doers, because He is just. All His Names are Exalted. His Blessings are Magnificent. He does not do the least injustice to His creatures, rather, man does injustice to himself.

Allah (s.w.t.)'s own words bear testimony to this: *Then he who has done an atoms weight of good shall see it and he who has done an atoms weight of evil shall see it - 99:7-8.*

There are other ayahs in the Holy Book to this same effect giving detailed explanations of all matters. Falsehood cannot come in front of, nor behind It. It is a Book revealed by the Almighty Praiseworthy Allah. "

The Imam (asws) bent down his head for a while and said, "O Mufaddal! Mankind is perplexed and bewildered, blind, infatuated in their perverseness, followers of their own lustful desires. They have eyes but do not see, they have tongues but are mute and do not understand. They have ears but do not hear. They are happy in their shameful depravity. They presume that they are well-guided. Yet they are diverted from the rank of rational beings. They feed on the vegetation of' polluted dirty people. They deem themselves safe from a sudden visitation of death and the retribution of deeds. Alas! How ill fated are these people!"

This moved me to tears, and the Imam (asws) comforted me by saying that I was saved, because of having accepted the faith and the recognition (marifat), and was granted salvation.

ANIMAL WORLD

Imam (asws) continued, "I shall now speak to you about the animal world, so that you may have as much information regarding it as you have about the rest.

Just consider the physical composition and the construction underlying their build. They are not as hard as stone, for had they been so, they could not have been able to perform actions, nor are they soft, for in that case they could not have reared up their heads or stood erect by themselves without a prop.

They are composed of such pliable muscles as bend and double up. They are supported by hard bones which are gripped by the muscles and which are tied together by tendons with each other. Covering these bones and muscles is their skin which extends over the whole body.

The wooden dolls with rags wound round them tied by strings and with a varnish of gum over the whole, serve as an excellent example. Let the wood stand for the bones, the rags for muscles, the strings for tendons and the varnish for the skin.

If it is possible in the case of living and moving beings to come into existence by themselves, it should be reasonably expected to happen in the case of these lifeless figures. And if it is impossible in the case of these toys, it is even more preposterous in the case of animals.

Then look at the animals' bodies in depth. They are composed of muscles and bones like the human beings. They are endowed with eyes and ears, so as to enable men to get work from them. They would not have served man's purpose if they had been blind and deaf. They are deprived of the faculties of intellect and reason, so that they may remain subservient to men and should not disobey even when subjected to intolerably heavy labour and burden.

It could also be said that human slaves who possess intellect and reason also obey their masters despite the hard and laborious burdens upon them. The reply to this is that these kinds of men are few in number. Most the slaves are unwilling workers while the animals are obedient even under heavy burdens

If man had to do the work of a single camel or a mule, it would have required several men causing a disruption in other areas. These simple tasks would have taken all of the manpower without leaving any free for arts and various other professions. Men would have suffered a strain.

Just consider the compositions of the following three kinds of living beings, and the merits with which they are endowed.

Man, having been ordained to possess intellect and reason to undertake such professions as carpentry, masonry, smithy, sewing etc., has been endowed with broad palms with thick fingers to enable him to grasp all types of tools necessary for these professions.

Carnivorous animals, having been ordained to live on game, have been gifted with soft palms with claws capable of being drawn in. They are suitable for hunting but unfit for professional arts.

Herbivorous animals having been ordained neither for professional arts nor for hunting, have been gifted, some with slotted hoofs to save them from the hardness of the ground while grazing, while others have solid hooves to be able to squarely stand on the ground for better fitness as beasts of burden

Carnivorous animals are equipped with sharp fangs, hard claws, and wide mouths to serve as tools for hunting. If such claws were given to herbivorous animals, they would have been useless; for they neither hunt nor catch flesh. And if the carnivorous animals were given hooves instead of claws, they would have been unable to obtain their food required for nourishment. Don't you see that both these kinds of animals are gifted with exactly the things appropriately in accordance with their need - and, therein lies their survival.

Now look at the beasts and see how they follow their mothers. They neither need to be carried nor to be nurtured as is the case with the human babies. This is so because the mothers of those young ones do not possess the tools which the mothers of human babies possess. Human mothers possess kindness, love and the knowledge of the art of nurture with specialized hands and fingers to lift them. Babies of the animals are made as to help themselves in all types of work.

You will find the same in birds, for example, the young ones of hen, partridge and grouse begin to pick up corn and move about as soon as hatched from eggs. Birds whose young ones are weak, without the strength to stand, for example those of the wild and domestic pigeons, have mothers with extra maternal instinct, so that they bring to their young one's mouths nourishment garnered by them in their crops.

Such feedings continue until chicks can fend for themselves. The pigeons don't have a large brood like the hens, to enable the females to rear them up adequately without starving them. Everyone thus receives a due share from the bounty of the Almighty All Knowing Allah.

Just see how the legs of the animals are created in pairs to enable them to move easily. Had they not been created as such it would have caused great difficulty. The moving animal lifts up one foot while resting the other one on the ground. Two legged animals lift one and get support from the other. Four legged animals lift one pair and rest on the other, on the opposite sides.

If four legged animals had lifted the pair of legs on the same side, balancing on the other would have been difficult, just as a chair cannot stand on two front legs. The front leg of the right side and the hind leg of the left side are lifted together, and vice versa, for steady locomotion.

Don't you see that a donkey drives a grindstone in addition to carrying burdens, seeing that the horse is allowed comparative rest and comfort? And the camel does so much work, which cannot be accomplished by a number of men.

What would have been the case if it had declined to obey? It submits to even a child. How does the bull submit to its master plowing the fields with the yoke on its neck? The thoroughbred horses rush into sword-blades and spears like their masters during battles. A single person is able to look after a flock of sheep. If the sheep were to go astray, each one on its own way, how could anyone have been able to find them?

Similarly, the other species of animals are subservient to man, why? This is because they do not possess any intellect, or any power to reason out matters. Had they possessed intellect, they would have refused to perform a good deal of man's requirements.

The camel would have declined to submit, and the bull would have mutinied against its master, the sheep would have got scattered, and so on. If the beasts of prey possessed intellect and reason, they would have contested for materials of food with men. Who could have stood against them if they joined forces against man's requests?

Don't you see how they are prevented from so doing? They fear the habitats of men and flee from him, instead of man fearing them. They do not come out during the daytime in search of food, but at night. They fear men with all their majestic awesomeness without having suffered any harm or warning from him. If this had not been ordained so, they would have come jumping into human habitats and made their lives miserable.

The dog, among the beasts, is endowed with a special trait, loyalty to its master, his service and his safeguard. It keeps watch during dark nights, roaming about the premises safeguarding against burglars. It is prepared to lay down its life to save him and his flocks. Such is its loyalty to its master. It can put up with hunger and pain for its master's sake.

Why is the dog created on this pattern, except that it should serve to guard man, with its strong teeth, stout claws, a frightful back, why? It is to frighten the burglars and to prevent them from approaching the goods entrusted to its care.

Look as the faces of the animals and see how they are shaped. You will see that they have their eyes accommodated in the front, lest they strike a wall or fall into a pit. You will find their mouths cleft under the snout. If they were like those of men, they would not have been able to pick up anything from the ground. Don't you see that man does not pick up his food with his mouth? He does so with his hands.

This is a peculiar merit granted to man in comparison with other feeders. Since the animals did not possess such hands to enable them to pick up grass, the under part of the snout was cleft to enable them to pick up grass and chew it. It is further helped with lengthened lips to reach out to farther as well as nearer things.

Consider the tails of animals and the benefits ordained therein. It is a sort of covering for their excretory privities. It also helps them keep off flies and mosquitoes that settle on the dirt on their bodies. Their tails are patterned after the fans with which to drive away flies and mosquitoes. They also get relief by constantly wagging their tails. These animals stand on all fours, they have no occasion to move them about, they therefore, feel relieved by wagging their tails.

There are other benefits as well which human imagination is incapable of grasping and which are known only when the need arises. Among these benefits, the tail is the most handy weapon to extricate it when it gets stuck in the mud. The tail hair may also be used to advantage by men. The trunk of such animals is made flat by lying on all four legs to facilitate riding and copulation because of the situation of their relevant parts.

ELEPHANT

Consider the trunk of an elephant and the cleverness in its design. It serves the purpose of taking in food and water to the stomach, like the human hand. Without it the elephant cannot lift anything from the ground, since its neck is not long enough, which it may stretch forward like the animals.

In the absence of a long neck it has been given in its place a long trunk so that it may extend it and meet its need. Who has given it an organ to compensate for the absence of a missing one? Surely, He Who is so very Compassionate on His creatures. And how can this take place without set Design, as asserted by the perverse naturalists and atheists?

To the objection as to why it has not been endowed with a neck similar to that of the other animals, the reply is that the head and the ears of the elephant being very heavy would have caused great strain, even rupture, so its head is joined directly to the body to protect it against that contingency and instead thereof the nose is constructed to serve all those purposes it needs, including those of feeding.

GIRAFFE

Just consider the makeup of the giraffe and the distinct nature of its organs resembling certain other animals. Its head resembles that of a horse, the neck that of a camel, the cleft hoof' of a cow, and its skin that of a leopard.

Some ignorant people have supposed that this results from the union of several kinds of animals. These ignorant people say that different species of land animals come to the watering place and one from a certain species had sexual encounter with one from the other species, resulting in such an offspring that is a combination of all of the species.

To say such a thing is to show one's ignorance, and lack of the understanding of the Almighty Allah, glory be to Him. No animal enters into sexual union with animals of other species. No union takes place between a horse and a she-Camel or a camel and a cow. Sexual union can take place only between animals of similar shape, for example a horse and a she-ass resulting in a mule, or a wolf with a badger resulting in a hybrid.

Moreover, it never happens that the offspring of such a union can borrow one organ from one of the other mate. A giraffe has one organ resembling that of a horse, another that of a camel, another hoof that of a cow. But you see that a mule has its head, ears, back, tail and hoof midway between those of a donkey and a horse, so is its cry midway between neighing and braying. This argument adequately shows that a giraffe is not the offspring of the union of desperate species, but is one wonder of the wonderful creation of the Almighty Allah, demonstrating His All Encompassing Authority.

It should also be known that the Creator of the numberless species of animals creates some organs similar and some dissimilar as He likes. He adds in the composition whatever He Wills and curtails there from whatever He Wills. This is so that His dominance may be demonstrated and that nothing can hinder Him in anything He Wills.

Why is its neck long and what advantages do accrue to it there from? The advantage lies in enabling it to reach up to the leaves and fruits of the tall tress for its nourishment where it lives, dwells, and it is born and has its grazing places, the dense forests.

MONKEY

Just consider the creation of the monkey and the similarity that subsists between its organs and those of man with, the head, shoulders, chest and the internal organs.

Moreover, it is gifted with brain and intellect because of which it understands the signals and the directions of its master. It generally copies man's activities as it sees him. It is very close to man in its qualities, traits and the way it is made.

It should serve as an admonition to man that he should bear in mind that in his nature and material he is animal-like, resembling them so closely and if he were not gifted with brain, intellect and speech, he would have been just like animals.

There are certain additions in the make up of the monkey which differentiates it from man e.g., the mouth, the long tail, the hair covering the whole body. These differences, however, would not have hindered it to become human, if it had been gifted with reason, intellect and speech faculties like man. The real line of boundary between it and man, as such, is due only the facilities of reason, intellect and speech.

ANIMAL SKIN

Just consider the Mercifulness of Almighty Allah towards these animals in giving their bodies a covering with different kinds of hair to protect them against winter hardships. And they have been gifted with hooves, cleft and uncleft, or padded feet to protect them. They have neither hands, nor palms nor fingers to spin and weave, and so their clothing is made part of their bodily build to serve them all through life without renovating and changing.

Man, however, possesses hands and skill to weave cloth and spin thread. He makes cloth and from time to time changes it with many advantages to him. Among them, he is kept busy with manufacturing his clothing and is thereby saved from harmful activities and idleness. He puts off his clothing whenever he wants to be at home. He can make various kinds of dresses for the pleasure he gets in their change. He prepares socks and shoes by way of fine industry to protect his feet. The labourers, and the traders thereby get their livelihood and the livelihood of their families. These different kinds of hair serve the animals as clothing; while their hooves and padded feet by way of footwear.

BURYING THE DEAD

Just consider the trait of animals, namely, the concealment of the dead bodies when they die just as men bury their dead.

Not a single dead body of the beasts and animals is seen. They are not so far as to be overlooked. In fact their population is greater than that of men.

Look at the flocks of deer, the wild oxen, the wild ass, the wild goats and the stags and also the different species of the animals and beasts like the lion, the badgers, the wolves, the leopards etc., and the varieties of insects living inside the bowels of the earth and moving on its surface, in the deserts and the mountains, and similarly the flight birds like crows, the partridge, the ducks, the cranes, the pigeons, the birds of prey. None of their corpses do we see except the few that the hunter gets as game or those that are devoured by beasts. As a matter of fact when these animals get a feeling of approaching death, they hide themselves in some secret place and die there.

Look at the arts that man has learnt from these animals. Its first example was when he saw two crows fighting, one killing the other and then burying its dead body, whence Qabeel learnt to dig and conceal his brother Habeel's corpse. That was undertaken under the guidance of Almighty Allah. These animals were given the instinct to save man from the affliction of those troubles and epidemics which would have followed.

ANIMAL INSTINCT

Consider the instincts with which they have been naturally gifted by the Almighty Allah through His infinite Mercy so as not to leave any creature deprived of His compassion.

The Ozan (deer) swallows up a snake but it does not drink water, however intense its thirst, for fear of the poison circulating in its body because of water, which may kill it. It roams about water tanks. It cries because of the intensity of thirst but does not touch water for fear of death. You see the great restraint that these animals possess in regard to intense thirst because of the fear or harm to an extent that a rational wise man is unable to undertake.

The fox, when it does not get food in any other way, feigns death with its belly inflated to deceive birds into believing it to be dead. As soon as the birds come round it to devour the apparent dead body, it attacks them and makes a hearty meal of them.

Now, say, who has given this skill to the speechless irrational fox? Surely, He Who has taken upon Himself the responsibility of feeding it. As the fox cannot undertake those activities which other beasts can, e.g., direct attack on the victim, it has been gifted with skill and cleverness as means for livelihood.

The Dolphin needs birds as victims. It catches a fish and kills it so that it may keep floating; on the water while hiding underneath it, stirring the water all the time to keep its own body hidden. As soon as a bird pounces upon the fish, the dolphin pounces on it and takes hold of the bird. By this skill it gets its victim."

PYTHON AND THE CLOUD

I then requested for an account of a python and the cloud.

Imam (asws) replied that the cloud is a sort of an angel to get hold of its python wherever it may find it, just as the magnet stone gets hold of iron. It does not raise its head from the earth because of the fear of the cloud except in summer when the sky is clear without a trace of cloud and then too only once.

I asked, "Why is the cloud made overlord of the python to get hold of it wherever it may find it?"

The Imam (asws) replied, "To save men from its harm."

ANT

I said, "Master! You have given an account of the animal world so fully as to serve as an eye opener for everyone. Kindly give some account of the ants and the birds."

The Imam (asws) said, "Look at the jaws of this little ant. Do you find any deficiency therein affecting its benefit? Where has this propriety and measure come from? Surely the same wisdom and design which has gone into the build of all creation, big or small.

Just see how the ants gather together to gather food for themselves. You will find that when several ants mean to carry a grain to their homes they resemble several men engaged in carrying home their corn. The ants in fact bring in effort and activity which men cannot do. Do you not see how they help each other in carrying the grain like men? They break the grain into pieces lest they should sprout and become useless for their purpose. In case the grains get moist, they spread them to get dry. The ants burrow their holes at elevated places, away from the danger of flooding.

All these activities, however, are without the intervention of reason, purely instinctive, with which their constitutions are endowed with, by the Kindness of the Almighty Allah.

SPIDER

Just look at the insect called 'Lais' (a kind of spider), generally called the lion of' the flies. How great skill, brilliance and mildness it has been endowed with for its livelihood. You will see that when it has a feeling of the approach of a fly, it ignores him for a while as if the spider itself is a lifeless body. When it feels that the fly is put off guard and is altogether unaware of its presence, it begins moving towards it in slowing step by step motion till it gets near enough to catch it, upon which it pounces and gets hold of it. Getting hold of it, it embraces it with its whole body to prevent its escape. It holds on until it feels the fly to have weakened and its limbs to have relaxed, when it turns to it and devours it. This is the way it lives on.

The ordinary spider weaves its web and uses it as a trap for the catching of flies. It sits hidden within it. As soon as it fly is trapped, it pounces upon it, cutting it into pieces. It lives on like this. Just see how this weak insect has been gifted with the instinct to catch its prey which man cannot do without using artifice and implements.

Do not find fault with anything, for everything has a lesson to teach just like the ants etc. A fine meaning is often expressed by an insignificant thing without depreciating its value just as gold is not depreciated if it is weighed against iron weights.

BIRD

Just consider the physical build of the bird as it was ordained that it would fly high in the air. It has been gifted with a light body and a comparatively compact constitution. It has only two feet instead of four, four fingers instead of five, only one orifice for excretion instead of two. It is gifted with a sharp chest to cut through the air just as a boat is built to cut through water. It has long stiff feathers on its sides and tail to help it fly high. The whole body is covered with feathers to get filled with air for high flights.

Since it was ordained for it that its nutrition will consists of grains and flesh which it will swallow without mastication, teeth have been missed from its build and a stiff beak to seek food has been given to it with which it can pick up food material. It is not injured in picking up nor broken by nibbling flesh. Since it has no teeth, but takes in grains and raw flesh, a great deal of heat is created in its stomach which serves to digest its food without the need for chewing. It is just an example that the seeds of grapes pass out of man's stomach as such while they are completely digested in the bird's stomach. Birds have been so constituted as to lay eggs rather than give birth to young ones so that they may not have any burdens to bear in flight due to the fetus in the womb staying to be fully developed.

Everything in its build has been so created as to be fully appropriate to its situation in life. It was also ordained that the birds that had to fly in the air should sit for a week, or two weeks, or three weeks on the eggs to bring forth their chicks. They then turn to them with their entire attention. It has a beak large enough to bring up its young ones with food on which it can subsist.

Who has entrusted it with tasks of first filling up its beak with grains picked up from the field, and then to place the same into the beak of the young ones? Why does it take all that trouble although it has no faculty of reasoning nor has it any expectations which man entertains about his young ones - honour, survival of name, and inheritance, etc. This is an activity which demonstrates that it is a special blessing to its chick under a special dispensation of the Almighty Allah which the bird itself cannot know, nor reason out. And what is it? It is an arrangement for the survival of the race.

HEN

Just look at the hen and see how anxious it is to lay the eggs and to bring forth the chicks although it has neither any particular nest nor the eggs from the same stock. It clucks, expands its feathers; it gives up its nourishment, unless it is given eggs to sit on and to bring forth the chicks, why? In order to preserve the race. Had it not been instinctively ordained, who could have obliged it for the preservation of the race, although it has no intellectual or reasoning faculty?

Just look to the composition of the egg and the white and the yellow matters inside it. One part is for the chick to be constituted while the other is to serve it as its nourishment till such time as it leaves the egg. Just see how the wisdom underlying it. The formation of the chick was to be carried on safely within the shell without allowing any exterior disturbances. Its nourishment was provided within it which is sufficient till it gets out. A person who is imprisoned securely without any able to approach him is provided with enough food to suffice him till his release.

BIRD'S CROP

Just consider the bird's crop and the wisdom behind it. The stomach is approached by a narrow tube to allow nourishment to reach it in small quantities. Without the crop, the grain would have taken time to reach the stomach. The bird in its far-sightedness fills up its crop hastily. Its crop is constructed on the pattern of the knapsack (bag carried on one's back) except it is suspended in front of it. In this way it may fill it up hastily with whatever it gets, then slowly transfers it to the stomach.

There is another advantage in the crop. Certain birds have to transfer food material to their young ones. The crop helps them to transfer it easily.

BIRD'S FEATHERS

Some people of this materialistic school claim that the diverse hues and the physical build of the birds are merely clue to the compounding of elements and humours in varied proportions. They are not due to any particular design.

Can this irrational concoction bring forth such ornamentation which you see in the peacock or the partridge and their perfect symmetry as if some artist has painted it with a fine brush without any flaw? If these artistic models came into being without the Almighty Artist, how could this symmetry and uniformity be maintained?

Just look closely at the feathers of a bird, you will find it like cloth woven with fine strings. One hair is interwoven with another just as one piece of thread is interwoven with another.

Look at its composition. If you open it, it opens up without being split to allow air to be filled in and to allow the bird to fly when it likes. Within the feather you will find a stout stick covered with hair-like material so that because of its stoutness, it holds them. The stick is hollow within so as not to be a burden to the bird and hinder its flight.

LONG-LEGGED BIRDS

Have you ever seen the long-legged bird and ever thought of the advantage it has of the long legs?

It is often found at comparatively shallow water. You will find it is for keeping watch at the spot standing on its long legs. It keeps watching the movements in the water. When it finds anything edible, it slowly moves to it and catches hold of its victim. If its legs had been shorter, its belly would have touched the water as it moved towards its victim causing the water to stir and it would fail to catch its prey. It has therefore been gifted with two long props to fulfill its need without any obstacle.

PROVISION OF FOOD

Just consider the other parts of intelligent design within the make up of the birds. You will find every long-legged bird possesses a long neck as well to enable it to pick up its food from the ground. It sometimes happens that a long beak is made to serve the purpose of a long neck leading to the required facilities.

Do you not see that whatever creation you consider, you will find it exact and full of wisdom?

Look at those herbs which these birds seek after during the day. It never happens that they don't find them or that they are scattered about instead of collected in one place. They obtain them by searching and moving about. This same situation prevails in the case of other creatures.

Glory be to the Almighty Allah who has apportioned sustenance and arranged it in different ways to supply it.

Provisions have not been arranged in such a way that they are either completely out of reach or so easily obtained that no effort is required. If the food had been gathered in one place in limitless quantities, then the animals would have become gluttanous and never leaving the place. This would have led to their destruction. The same applies to man. Because of abundance, he succumbs to conceit and pride which result in mischief and evil doings."

NIGHT BIRDS

The Imam (asws) asked me, "Do you know about the birds like the owl and bat, which only come out at night, and search about for their food material?"

I (Mufaddal) replied, "I do not know."

Imam (asws) said, "The food of these consists of those varied kinds of insects scattered in the atmosphere, e.g. the mosquitoes, the moth, the locust-shaped insects and spiders etc. They are always present in the atmosphere, no place is free from them. When you light a lamp at night on the roof or in the compound, many of such kind of insects gather around it.

Where do they come from? Surely from near about they come. If anyone says that they come from the forests and fields, he will be answered with the query as to how they reach so soon and how can they see the lamp lit inside a building surrounded by many other buildings, while as a matter of fact they take no time to come round the lamp. It is clear from this that all these are scattered everywhere in the atmosphere and the birds that come at night catch hold of them and feed on them.

See how nourishment is arranged for the birds that come out at night by means of such insects, scattered in the atmosphere. Try to understand the purpose of the creation of such living creatures, lest someone may consider that they are created in vain without any advantage.

The bat is a strange creature, midway between a bird and an animal, in fact more akin to an animal, with two protruding ears, teeth and fine hair. It gives live birth to its young ones, whom it feeds on its milk. It urinates and excretes. It moves on all fours. All these traits are contrary to those of birds. It comes out only at night and feeds on insects scattered in the atmosphere.

Some say it does not eat anything; but lives only on cool air as nourishment. This is incorrect for two reasons, for it urinates and excretes, which presupposes solid food. Then it possesses teeth, if it did not have to eat, the teeth would be useless, whereas there is nothing; in creation which is useless.

This creature has well-known merits. Their excreta is mixed with other things. Its strange make up is in itself a wonder. It flits about as it wills for its own benefit - a sign of the Great Authority of the Almighty Allah.

The weaver bird builds its nest on the trees sometimes. If it sees a big snake aiming at its nest, it gets worried. It looks about for means of safety. As soon as it comes across a thorny seed, it picks it up and throws from above into the open mouth of the snake. The snake begins to writhe and convulses into death.

If I had not spoken to you of this, could you have imagined that a thorny seed could have such benefits, or could anyone think that a bird, big or small, could hit upon such a plan? Learn a lesson from this. There are many other things with unknown benefits which remain hidden unless they are explained in their minute details.

BEE

Just consider the bee and the concerted efforts to produce honey and the hexagonal hive, and the subtleties of instinct that subsists therein. You will find it extremely wonderful, when you consider its workings. You will find their manufacture to be magnificent and of fine use for men.

And when you look at the artisan, you will find it devoid of intelligence, incapable of knowing itself, what to say of others. In this is a clear proof that the exactness in skill and brilliance is not due to the bee but to the Mastery of Him Who has created it on such pattern and appointed it to the service of men.

LOCUSTS

Just look at the locust—how weak, yet how strong. No one would be able to protect himself against a swarm of locusts, if they invade a town.

Don't you know that if any of the monarchs of the whole earth comes cut with his armies and dependents to fight the locusts, he would not succeed?

Is not this an argument demonstrative of the Power of the Almighty Allah, that the strongest of His creation would be unable to withstand the attack of the weakest of His creatures? Look at how they cover the entire earth like a flood, spreading over the mountain, the desert, the plain and the town, all in one, so that its swarm intercepts even the sight of the sun.

Now calculate how many years would have been required to manufacture such a swarm with the hand. The Almighty Allah has given hereby another proof of His Power, which nothing can minimize and to which nothing can be redundant.

FISH

Just consider the fish and circumstances under which it is ordained to lead its life. It has no legs, since its residence is in water and it does not need to walk. It has no lungs, as it cannot breathe. It is kept under the surface of water.

Instead of legs, it is endowed with stout fins with which it pierces the water on both sides; just as a boatman uses two oars. It has a covering of thick scales, interlocked with each other like the links of a coat of armor to protect itself. It has a penetrating faculty of smell, as compensation for weak eyesight blurred by water. It smells its material from a distance and goes towards it. How else could it have learnt the whereabouts and nature of the food material? And, know too, that it has orifices all along the mouth to the ears, through which water passes and gives it the same refreshing exuberation as is derived by other animals by breathing in fresh cool morning breeze.

Now, consider its reproductive characteristics. The number of eggs inside the fish is beyond computation. The reason is to increase the food potentials of other living beings, for most others live on fish at the edges of water pools, amidst the bushes. As soon as a fish passes by, they pounce upon it. Since the beasts, the birds, man and even other fish prey upon the fish, it has been ordained to have a large number of eggs so has to keep up its numbers and not disappear.

In order to get an idea of the vast wisdom of the Almighty Allah look at the diversity of the animals, the shells, the aquatic life and the different species of fish and the nature of the knowledge each creature possesses. They are limitless in number and all of their merits can never be known. Man can only happen to understand certain aspects due to different situations arising that allow him to gain knowledge regarding that particular merit.

As an example the Cochineal, the colour of it was learnt by men through a dog roaming on the sea-shore, having found and eaten Halzoon (an insect possessing colour). Its mouth got coloured. The colour fascinated the people who began using the cochineal insect as a dye. There are several other things of which the characteristics become known from time to time to the people."

It was afternoon. My Master rose for prayers, telling me to come to him early next morning.

I came back home doubly pleased with the gift of instruction in knowledge I had received from him.

Chapter Four

THIRD SESSION

ENVIRONMENT

I presented myself early on the morning of the third day, and upon obtaining permission I entered and sat down.

Imam (asws) began, "O Mufaddal! I have explained to you in detail about the creation of man and the subtle design of the Almighty Allah that has gone into his perfection and the lessons to be learnt from the altering of circumstances. I have also discussed regarding the animal world.

I shall now take up the account of the atmosphere, the sun, the moon, the stars, the sky, day and night, summer and winter, the winds, the four fundamentals, rain, the rocks, the mountains, the plant kingdom, the date tree, and the common trees, pointing out the signs contained therein and the lessons to be learnt from there.

SKY

Look at the colour of the sky and see how appropriate is the design! This particular colour is the most appropriate tonic compared with all the other colours. Even the physicians direct a man to gaze on the green hue or on some other darker hue in case of some ailment of the eye. Efficient physicians direct a person with a weakened eyesight to gaze on in a basin of green colour, filled with water.

Just see how the Almighty Allah has created the sky with a green colour inclined to be dark, so as not to cause, by repeated looks, some imperfection. This same characteristic which people have found out as a result of thinking and experimentation is a self-existent characteristic, so that those who would, learn a lesson there from, and the heretics - may Allah (swt) destroy them, go astray.

SUNRISE AND SUNSET

Consider the rising and the setting of the sun in the production of the day and night. Without sunrise, all businesses of the world would come to a stop. The world would be sunk in darkness with no possibility for work or livelihood. There would be no relish in life without the pleasant effects of sunlight. The benefits of sunrise are obvious indeed and need not be discussed in detail.

Now just consider the sunset. If it did not set, men would have no comfort nor any rest. Men inevitably need to rest and comfort to recuperate the faculties of digestion and assimilation, and to soothe and relax the nerves of the body.

Their greed, by persistent work, would have caused serious bodily disturbances for many are so that unless the night conceal them, they would enjoy no comfort and rest in their pursuit of livelihood and the accumulation of wealth.

Perpetual sunshine would have heated the earth with repercussions on the lives of the animals and plants. The Almighty Allah has, therefore, ordained that there shall be periods of sunshine and darkness, like the lamp which is lit up as the household needs and it is put out when not needed, to give them comfort and rest. Light and darkness are opposed to each other and yet both are made subservient to the interests of the world's betterment and improvement.

FOUR SEASONS

Then consider the four seasons of the year which occur as a result of the elevation and inclination of the sun and the benefits and planning contained within. The trees and plants are renewed between the vital two periods of the sun's movement.

The condensation of vapour in the air causes clouds and rain. The animals get their bodies re-invigorated in this season. There is an upsurge of vital heat in the summer as well with the production of the material which matures in winter. The plants get flowers and fruit in this season. The animals come into heat.

The air is heated in summer which leads to the ripening of fruit. The waste products of the body get accentuated. The earth gets dried up and becomes fit for building and other performance.

Air is purified in winter, ailments are negotiated. Physical bodies become healthy. Night gets longer and thus aids in the performance of certain tasks because of the longer periods.

The air in this season suits other performances as well. It would take an enormous amount of time to discuss all of these in detail.

SUN

Now consider the motion of the sun through the twelve Zodiac belts to complete a year and the skill underlying it. This is the period that comprises the four seasons - Winter, Summer, Autumn and Spring, in their completeness. Grains and fruits ripen during this annual movement of the sun to meet human needs and the cycle of development continues on in a repetitive cycle.

Don't you know that the sweep of this sun across the heavenly belt, from the Pisces belt back to it, constitutes one year? The year has continued as the calculating measures of time since the beginning of the world in all past ages. People calculate the periods of life-spans, loans, contracts and other business matters by it. It is with the movement of the sun that one year is complete and a correct estimate of time is established.

Just see how the sun sheds its light on the world and with what wisdom has been ordained in it. If it shone only at one spot of the globe constantly, without changing its place, the benefits of its rays would not penetrate in all directions.

It has, therefore, been so designed that it rises from the East in the morning. Moving constantly, extending its light from side to side till it goes on to the West to shed its light on objects which failed to receive it in the morning, so no corner will remain without the benefit and purpose it is meant to serve.

If for a whole or a part of the year the situation changed to the contrary, you can imagine the plight of human beings. In fact what chance would they have to survive at all?

Does not man observe such magnificent planning, wherein his own plans would utterly fail? They function automatically without negligence, and do not lag behind the time regulated for the management of the world's organization and maintenance.

MOON

There is a sign revealed by the Almighty Allah in the creation of the moon. People in general calculate months on its basis, but the year is not correctly established by it. Its motion does not comprehend the changes of season nor the times of the blossoming and the ripening of the crops. That is why lunar months and years differ from solar months and years. The lunar months change, so that sometimes the same month has reference to the summer and sometimes to winter. So is the case with other months. For example, the month of Muharram may occupy a period in summer sometimes, in the rainy season at other times and in winter at yet another time. This shows that the lunar and solar months continue to change and do not correspond to each other.

Consider why the moon shines at night and the wisdom underlying it. The living beings need coolness born of darkness in order to get rest and comfort. Complete absence of light and pitch darkness would not have any merit due to the impossibility for work of any kind. Men need to undertake some work for want of leisure during the day. It may be that due to extremes of heat, he may work in the glimmer of the moon, for example, agriculture, milking. wood cutting etc. The moonlight helps men to work for their livelihood whenever they are so disposed. The wayfarers find fascination in their travels. Moonrise is ordained for different parts of the night, which it is made less luminous than the sun at the same time, lest people start working in the same way as they do during the day without resting even unto death.

In the different phases of the moon, its appearance as a crescent, its disappearance during the nights at the end, its waxing and waning and its eclipses, there are particular indications that all these changes are ordained for the benefit of the universe by the Almighty Creator Allah, which can serve as instruction for any man disposed to avail such instruction.

STARS

Just consider the stars and their distinctive orbits. There are some among them which do not budge from the positions appointed for them. There are others which move from zone to zone and have their distinctive velocities. Each one of them has two velocities - one due to the cosmic motion in the direction of the west, the other its intrinsic velocity in the direction of the east.

This is comparable to the two velocities of an ant on the upper piece of the grindstone. The grindstone moves to the right and the ant in the opposite direction. In such a case the ant will have two velocities—one its own direction, the front direction and the other unintended, along with the grindstone.

Now just inquire from these people who claim that these stars have come into being by themselves without the Design of the Almighty Designer, as to what was the hindrance in their all becoming stationary or moving bodies?

Creation without Creator presumes a single pattern, why should there occur two different movements on a definite pattern and quantum? All this clearly demonstrates that the movement of the two categories of stars as it subsists at present, is the result of a definite Purpose, Design and Brilliance, not something meaningless as these materialist atheists claim.

If an objection is raised as to why some stars are stationary while others possess motion, our answer shall be that in case all were stationary, the distinctive signs that are now revealed by their movements from zone to zone would be out of place. Many a secret is known by a knowledge of the events connected with the sun and other stars because of their movements in their respective orbits. The advantage now gained in the matter of crop season and even predictions etc., through the movements of a few stars at present, would be out of reach.

If all of them were to possess motion, their destination would have no outposts to be recognized. The movement of the moving planets in their appointed zones affords the necessary information, just as the rate of motion of a wayfarer as gauged by the measure of distances. In the absence of the measures of miles, or stage, an estimate of the rate of motion would be difficult.

Similarly, if all these stars were to possess motion and motions of different quantums at that, an estimate of the rate of their motion would have been impossible. Firstly because they are numberless beyond the computation of any computer or astronomer, and secondly because of their location—some in the east, others in the west, still others in the north and yet others in the middle or on the extremities or here, there and everywhere. Their zones would be equally impossible to fix, and thirdly because of the difficulty of all of them passing; through the twelve belts. It would then have been impossible to draw any distinctions, thereby the whole purpose of their motion and existence would have been nullified.

If they all moved with a uniform rate of motion, the objective underlying would have been made redundant.

An objection in that case from a critic would have been in place to the effect that a uniformity of motion on a single pattern indicates the absence of a Designer - a Creator, as we have deduced in proof of the Being of the Almighty Allah. It is thus quite obvious that their distinctive velocities, the changes and their movements being purposeful, are the working of Design and Discrimination.

Consider the stars that appear in certain parts of the year and disappear during the other parts of a year, for example, the Pleiades, the Orion, the pair of stars of the Sirius and the Canopus. If all of them appeared simultaneously, none could stand as a distinct symbol for men to recognize, to know and receive guidance, just as men deduce from the appearance and disappearance of the Orion and the Taurus. This appearance and disappearance of each at appropriate occasions was ordained for the benefit of men.

Just as the Pleiades were ordained to appear and disappear at different times for particular benefits of men, similarly the constellation of the Bear has been ordained for perpetual view, never to disappear, as it has another objective to serve, as a sign-post for men to seek their way through the unknown paths amidst forest and oceans. As the stars of' this constellation are ever in view, men look to them immediately when they need to know the path for any direction. Both these opposite phenomena serve human interests.

Besides, therein is the indication of time, for agriculture, horticulture, travel through land and sea. There is also intelligibility of other phenomena that have reference to different times, for example the rainfall, blowing of winds, the summer and the winter seasons.

Moreover, men find their way with their aid in travels through dreadful plains and fearful oceans during hours of dark nights. There are besides, a great many lessons to be learnt from these stars which now move forwards, some backwards in the direction of the Last or the West.

The heavenly bodies, the moon and the sun move very fast, and if they were nearer to us and their velocity would be felt exactly as it is, do you not think the eyes would have been dazzled by their brilliance and radiation, just as they are dazzled by the radiation of the lightning when it begins scintillating continuously, kindling the space between the earth and the sky like fire?

Another illustration of this is a house with its ceiling studded with many live candles revolving round the head with terrific speeds. The eyes will necessarily be corrupted throwing the beholders prostate on their faces. Just see how it has been ordained that they would move with their existing speeds at huge distances from us to protect our eyesight against damage and disease, while retaining their tremendous speed for the purpose they have to serve.

The stars are just bright enough to give light in the absence of the moon and to enable us to move about in their glimmer. Man sometimes needs to journey at night, and in the absence of their glow, he would have found it difficult to go on his way.

Just consider the kindness and creativity ordained in this creation. Darkness was also needed and a period is allocated therefore, with the addition of the glimmer, to serve the objectives we have dealt with.

UNIVERSE

Consider the universe together with its sun, moon, stars and Zodiac, which revolve perpetually in accordance with a definite decree and judgment to bring about numerous benefits to the inhabitants of the earth, diverse animal and vegetable kingdoms through the changes in the four seasons, the days and nights, which have been explained in detail to you. Can any man with a discerning mind think that such regulated plan and design on which depend the order and organization of the universe, can come about without the All Knowing Designer?

If someone says that mere chance has brought this about, why does he not say that same thing in connection with the Persian-wheel which he sees revolving, irrigating a garden planted with trees and vegetation? He sees all its component parts manufactured according to a definite plan, each part coupled with the other on a pattern to serve the needs of the garden and its contents.

And if he makes the same remarks about the Persian-wheel, then what opinion about him will people entertain on hearing his remarks? Surely this is a ignorant man with no intellect. Does he not see how the matter and the nature of the Persian-wheel, which is itself inert and devoid of intellect, would by itself come into being with perfect appropriateness to the requirements of the garden? Can any reasonable man admit it?

Will he deny it in the case of a wooden Persian-wheel comprising a little planning and ingenuity, that it is not a piece of workmanship planned and designed, and yet will be able to say that this stupendous universe which is full of projects beyond human imagination, functioning for the entire earth's surface and its contents, has come into being by mere chance without Skill, Design or Measure? Has man the means to see right if anything goes wrong with the sky, just as the wooden parts of machinery get out of order?

DAYS AND NIGHTS

Just consider the relative hours of the day and night. They are adjusted for the benefit of creation. The days or the nights do not exceed fifteen hours.

Do you know that if days were extended to a hundred or two hundred hours, the animal and plant life would have perished? Men would have continued to work on without stopping with consequent peril to life. The plant life would have withered away under the prolonged effect of heat of the daytime.

Similarly, if the night had been prolonged equally, all species of living beings would have been prevented from moving about and finding nutriment with consequent starvation. The plants would have lost their vital heat, delayed and perished, just as you see those plants which are so placed as to receive little sunshine.

HEAT AND COLD

Consider the heat and cold cycle of increase, decrease , and the resultant four seasons following one another in the world and functioning for our benefit. By which, the physical bodies get improved and renewed. This leads to their health and longevity, for in the absence of the effects of heat and cold alternatively, they would have suffered decadence, disintegration and emaciation.

The two (heat and cold) replace each other gradually and slowly. You will notice that the decreases giving place gradually to the corresponding increase of the other. If the one had suddenly erupted on the other, it would lead to serious damage, to an illness of the physical body, just as man may receive damage and illness, if he suddenly issues from a hot bath into a cold place. The Almighty Allah has ordained the gradual change of heat and cold to protect man from damage of suddenness of change.

If anyone claims that this gradualness in the advent of heat and cold results from the movement of the sun and its inclination affecting the duration of the day, he may be questioned as to the reason of the movement of the sun and its gradual inclination affecting gradualness. If he answers that it is due to the space of the Last and the West, he may be queried as to why it is so disposed. The questions on this line will continue to be repeated till he is obliged to admit the necessity of All Powerful, Purpose and Design.

Without heat, the hard bitter fruits would not have matured into succulent sweetness, used for relish, fresh or dry. Without cold, the stalks would not bear corn ears in such abundant produce to suffice for nutriment and seeding.

Don't you realize the benefits of heat and cold which, with all their merits are sources of trouble to the bodies as well? There is instruction for those who would ponder over this, and a proof that all this procedure is for the good of the universe and, the individuals thereof through the Design of the Almighty All Knowing.

Let me inform you of the blessings of air. Don't you see when it stops blowing, there is distress bordering on strangulation? Healthy persons begin ailing, the ailing get emaciated, the fruits get spoiled, vegetables get decayed, physical bodies get infected and corn gets tainted? This demonstrates that the blowing of air is for the good of creation by a Plan of the Almighty Omniscient.

Another characteristic of the air is sound. Sound is produced by the impact of two bodies, one upon the other. It is wafted to the ears by air. All men continue to speak part of the night or day in connection with the needs of daily business. If this speech had left its impression in the air as writing leaves an impression on paper, the whole atmosphere would have been filled with consequent uneasiness and perplexity. They would have needed a change in atmospheric air.

The Almighty Creator, Glory be to Him, has created such a mysterious medium, which retains the impression just for enough time to serve the needs of the people of the world and makes a clean state to get renewed for fresh impressions to be received by it.

This air is the foundation of the life of physical bodies. It supports life when we draw it in from without and allow it to contact the spirit within. This same air is the medium, for the transmission of sound waves to distant places. The same air carries fragrance from place to place. Just see how air wafts different kinds of scents and smells to your nose, it also carries heat and cold. The air in motion is wind which removes many a physical ailment. It transfers clouds form place to place for the general good by way of condensation and rain. It then accentuates them and they fritter away. It causes the plants to bring forth blossoms and fruits. It makes the nutrients soft and succulent. It cools water. It inflames the fires and it dries up dampness. In short, it supports and enlivens all things of the earth. Without this blowing air, vegetation would dry up, animal life would become extinct and everything would perish.

EARTH

Consider the four fundamental components created by the Almighty Allah to fulfil the purpose of their creation adequately. Among them is the earth and its expanse. How could it have sufficed for the human needs of housing, agriculture, meadows, forests, jungles, precious herbs and valuable minerals, if it were not so vast?

A person may dislike and condemn such treeless prairies and fearful desolateness and question their necessity. This is the abode of the beasts, their dwelling and feeding field. Men have a vast expanse to migrate if they are so disposed. Many a desolate plain has been converted into blossoming gardens and palatial buildings by permanent human settlement. If the earth were not so vast, men would have found themselves, as if walled in by narrow fortresses, for they would have been unable to leave their homes even if circumstances required them to do so.

Next, consider how the earth is so balanced as to serve as a fit habitat for all of creation. Man is enabled thereby to move about, get rest and comfort, engage in agriculture and business. If the earth were to tilt and incline it would have been impossible to rear up structures and to carry on trade and industry etc. Under such circumstances of constant quaking, their lives would have been far from pleasant. Just realize this from the earthquakes which last only a while and yet people affected by them fly from their homes. How could they, then, have got rest and comfort, in case the earth was to quake all the time?

If a critic questions as to why an earthquake occurs, he shall be replied that an earthquake and similar other calamities are in the nature of admonition and warnings for men to take heed against evil-doings. Similarly the calamitous troubles that befall their physical bodies and their properties are also for their improvement and betterment. If they become virtuous, the reward they would get in the Hereafter would exceed all earthly possessions in value. It sometimes happens that there is an immediate reward in this world, if such reward is in the interests of the generality of people.

The earth in its essence is cool and dry, and so are the stones. Can you imagine if the earth had been made a little more dry so as to harden like a stone? Could it have produced any vegetation on which the animal life depends? Could any agriculture have been possible or any kind of building been feasible? Don't you see that it possesses less cohesion than a stone? Pliability and softness from its essence are for the sake of reliability.

Another feature of the earth's constitution as ordained by Almighty Allah; Glorious is His Omnipotence, is its gradual slope from the north to the south. Why has Almighty Allah, Glory be to Him, Ordained it? Surely to allow the surplus water after irrigating the land, to flow to the sea, just as roof is made sloping from one side to other to prevent water collecting and to allow its easy passage. The land is made to slope for that reason. If it were not so, the whole earth might have been swamped with stagnant water causing a hindrance in business and road communications.

AIR

Similarly, if the air had not been provided in such abundance, men would have been suffocated because of the smoke and vapours congesting it. If the atmosphere had not been so vast, it could not have served as medium for light and heavy clouds, which now gradually gather up by absorption of water which has already been explained in detail.

FIRE

So is the case of fire. Had it been as abundant as water and air, it would have consumed everything in the world. It is of benefit in man as an undertaking and as such it has been enshrined in wood. It can be used when the need arises. It is preserved by means of wood. It is not allowed to be extinguished altogether, but some of it is preserved. It is not required to be kept perpetually burning for that would have been very inconvenient. Nor is it so widespread as to consume all things in its vicinity. It is created in just the right measure to avoid being non beneficial.

It has another defining characteristic. It is meant only for the benefit of human beings. Human economy would have suffered a lot in the absence of fire. As for the animals, they have no use for it.

As the Almighty Allah has ordained its use for human beings alone, man has been endowed with palms and fingers so as to be able to light it up and make use of it, while the animals are not gifted with the corresponding parts. They are, however, enabled patiently to put up with the troublesome pangs of the stomach to save them from the disadvantages which man has to suffer in the absence of the fire.

Let me tell you a minor merit of fire, which is very valuable and worthwhile. This lamp which people light up to meet certain needs of the night as they want. Without it human life would have been comparable to burial in a grave. For how could one read, write, weave, sew, or stitch in the darkness of the night?

WATER

If this water had not been in such abundance flowing through springs, valleys and canals, it would have caused a great deal of inconvenience to the men, who need it for themselves, the watering of their animals, their agriculture, the plants and corn fields. At the same time the beasts, the birds or the fishes and aquatic living creatures dwelling in water would suffer a great deal.

There are other benefits for which you are aware of but are ignorant of their true value and merit. The whole animal and plant life of the entire earth's surface is subsistent on water. It is used in other forms of beverages to soften them for a pleasant relish. It serves to clean the dirt from the body as well as clothing. Earth is moistened with it to make it fit for moulding utensils etc. It is used in extinguishing fire in case it flares up to cause damage. Man gets refreshed after exhaustion and exertion. Similarly there are other objectives served by water, the great worth and value thereof can be known only in time of need.

If, after all of this, you still doubt the value of such abundance of water flowing in rivers and seas, know then that this same water is the abode of many species of aquatic animal life and fishes. This is the treasure-house of pearls, rubies, ambergris and various types of precious materials which are extracted from the rivers and seas.

Furthermore, it is a means of transport. It is a means of trade exchange between lands distant from each other. For example, from Iraq to China and vice versa and even within Iraq itself. Trade would have suffered without such a means of transportation. Trade would have been limited to local consumers or only to those places one could reach through the use of animals or carrying upon their backs. Their transport would have cost more than their production costs. No one would have ventured to transport them.

This would have led to two handicaps. Many articles of necessity would not have been available. Suppose the ingredients required for medicinal purposes were only available in the cities of Asia or Europe? If it had been transported on the backs of animals without the means of boats, then how would it have reached the shores of India and how would the people of India been able to benefit from it? Secondly those who gain their livelihood from the profits gained through transporting good would have lost their economic support.

The other benefits in cooking, warming the body, burying the moist substances and dissolving hard materials etc., are limitless that they cannot be recounted and their benefit is so obvious there is no need for detailed explanations.

RAIN

Consider the sky when it is clear and when it rains. They alternate in the interest of the world. Persistence of any one state would have caused disorder. Don't you see that when it starts raining continually, the vegetables and plants begin to rot. The bodies of animals get convulsions. The atmosphere is cold with consequent ailment, roads and paths get disrupted. When the sky remains clear for a long time, the earth is dried up, the vegetation withers up. Man is affected greatly. The air gets dryness with consequent diseases.

When they alternate thus regularly, the climate is equable. Each in turn compensates the detriment of the other. Everything goes right.

A critic may question as to why it was not ordained that there were no detrimental effects. The answer will be it is so ordained so man may be occasionally inconvenienced to keep him from evil-doing. A sick person, for instance, is administered bitter and unpalatable medicine to cure him. Similarly when man betakes himself to pride and conceit, he needs to be administered something that would inconvenience him to prevent him from mischief and to set him upon beneficence and improvement. If a monarch bestows favors upon his people, will the people not begin to admire and revere him? What comparison have they with the rain which is the source of nourishment and the flourishing state of all parts of the globe through its irrigation of corn fields?

Don't you see what a grand blessing is this little rain for mankind? Yet the people are heedless thereof. Often times when some little need of a man is frustrated, he begins grumbling and blustering. He prefers his petty need over the worth-while grand benefits. This is because he is unable to fully appreciate the merits of this grand blessing. Consider the wisdom underlying the rain, pouring down on high to irrigate the inclement highland as well. If it were to come from a corner, it would have left the highlands without provision for agriculture. The lands of artificial irrigation are less extensive. Rain water comprehends the whole of the earth. Often times the agriculture can be carried on in the vastness of deserts and mountainous regions with consequent abundance of grain. People are saved trouble of carrying water from one place to another. Many problems arise when one person alone possesses the only water source leaving the weaker party deprived and without sufficient sustenance.

It was ordained as a sprinkling upon the earth to allow time for it to soak in and to irrigate it. If it had come with sudden swiftness like a flood, it would not have soaked in. It would, in the form of a flood, have uprooted standing crops. It is, therefore, ordained to rain in mild showers, as to enable seed to sprout, the land to be irrigated and the standing crops to be refreshed.

There are other blessings in this downpour. It tempers the bodies, purifies the atmosphere to clear it of taint produced by stagnation. Garden plants are cured of the disease of jaundice and so on.

If a critic says, whether the rain does not sometimes cause heavy damage by its intensity or in the form of hailstorms, causing the crops to perish and the atmosphere to get unwholesome vapour with resultant diseases and troubles. The answer will be that this damage too is sometimes intended for the betterment of' man to prevent him from indulging in transgressions. The benefit that shall accrue to him in the improvement of his faith will outweigh the loss suffered in his worldly possessions.

MOUNTAINS

Look at these mountains formed of earth and stone, which the ignorant consider as useless and unnecessary. They embody remarkable advantages. Among them is the snow that falls and stays on their heights. Anyone can benefit from it. When it melts and gives rise to springs of gushing water and marvelous canals, herbs and plants that cannot grow in the plains and lowlands are produced. They have dens and caves for the horrible beasts of prey. They serve for the superstructure of fortresses as defense posts. They can be cut into dwellings. They are chiseled into grindstones. They contain mines of precious stones of diverse types. Besides these, they have other merits, which He alone Who created them in definite measure, knows by His Pristine Knowledge of all eternity.

Consider the different kinds of minerals which are obtained from the mines. For example, mortar, lime, gypsum, sulphurate of arsenicum, lead oxide, mercury, copper, tin, silver, gold, beryl, ruby, garnet and various kinds of rocks and so on giving rise to tar, vaseline, sulphur, kerosene, etc., which are used by the people. Is it then any mystery for a rational being that all these treasures have been laid for use by man, which he may mine as and when he needs them?

Men, however, are greedy and want to convert base materials into gold and silver. They spend efforts in that direction but mostly in vain. Their plans do not come to fruition. If these people had succeeded in their search of knowledge, it would have become general knowledge. Gold and silver would have been produced in such abundance that they would have lost their worth in men's eyes. The advantages gained through the mine business and commerce would have been lost, and neither the monarchs nor anyone else would have set any stores by wealth.

Nevertheless, men were given the knowledge to change copper into brass, and into glass, tin into silver and silver into gold, which does not do much harm. Just see that knowledge was given where there was not much harm, whereas that which was harmful has been withheld.

And when a man enters a mine he may find inside it unfathomable streams of flowing water and silvery rocks.

Consider the underlying design in this of the Almighty All Knowing. He (swt) wants to give men an idea of the vastness of His treasures and Command, so that they may know that if He (swt) Wills, He (swt) can bestow on us silver in the amounts equal to mountains. He (swt) can do it, however, there would be little gain because the abundance of gems would reduce their worth, as stated before. Few would benefit from it.

To further illustrate this point, suppose a man invents something new. For example, utensils or other commodities. They are worth-while, grand and precious, so long as they are in short supply and rare, but when they exceed the demand and reach every pocket, then their value is lowered and they become worthless. Everything is considered valuable so long as it is rare.

VEGETATION

Consider the plants and the varied needs they fulfill. Fruit is used in nutrition, dried hay as fodder for the animals, wood as fuel; the boards are used for carpentry of every kind. There are various benefits accruing from their bark, leaves, large and small roots and gum.

Consider the fruits we use for our nutrition. If they were to be found in one place instead of being suspended by branches which bear them, what a disruption would have been caused in our lives! Nutrition would have been available no doubt, but what about the valuable benefits we derive from wooden boards, dried hay and other parts we have mentioned.

Moreover, the joy that is afforded by the scenic beauty and freshness of vegetation is incomparably superior to the pleasures and merriment of the whole world.

GRAINS

Consider how agriculture is ordained to thrive. A hundred or so grains spring from a single seed. A single grain from a single seed would have been logical. Why then such multiplication? Surely to amplify the grain so that the same may serve as food to last till the next crop and also provide seed for the farmers.

Consider a monarch intending to populate a town. He plans to provide a certain quantity of grain which will be sufficient for the residents to serve as food till the next crop and as provision for seed. See how this plan is indicated in the scheme of the Almighty Allah, Glory be to Him, that agriculture should lead to such multiplication as to serve both the need for nutrition as well as that for seeding.

Similar is the case with the trees, vegetation and the date-tree. They generate abundant fruit. You see that there is a single root, but there are many off-shoots. Why? Surely for the purpose of propagating the progeny from the seeds after people have put them to their use. If there had been a single root without the branches shooting off in such abundance, it would not have been feasible to take off anything from it for sowing or any other business. In the case of a sudden calamity the original would have perished with no chance for another plant to replace it.

Consider the grains of pulses and bean. They all grow in pods as a protection against harm, till they mature to hardness, just as the placenta. The grains of wheat and other similar grains are arranged layer by layer in hard shells, pointed sharply at their ends like spears to keep off the birds and to increase the yield to the farmers.

If, a critic asks whether the birds do not get at the grains of wheat, etc, the reply to him will be that they do get the grains no doubt and it is so ordained for them, since the birds are also the creation of the Almighty Allah. He (swt) has ordained for them a portion of the produce of the earth. These grains are protected in these coverings, lest the birds should get complete possession of them leading to evident loss through wanton waste. In the absence of such protection the birds would have pounced upon the grains and made short work of them all. They would have suffered indigestion to their evident detriment. The farmers too, would have been at a loss. Therefore these protective coverings have been provided. The birds take just enough for their need of subsistence leaving the major portion for the use of mankind. Man has a greater right because of the labour put in by them, and man's need is greater than that of the birds.

PROPAGATION OF PLANTS

Consider the propagation of plants and various species of vegetation. They need nutrition as much as animals. However, they have no mouths to feed themselves, nor can they move about to acquire their food. Instead, they have been gifted with roots under the earth to receive their nutriment and to transmit it to their branches, leaves and fruit. The earth acts as their mother from which they receive their nutrition and their roots acts as their mouths to obtain their food, just as the young ones of the animals feed on the milk from their mother.

Don't you see the pegs and ropes tied tightly to the tents in order to prop them up straight so there is no fear of them falling or bending? Similarly, you will find every plant supported by its roots spreading in all direction. How could the massive trees and all date-palms stand steady against the storms?

Behold! The wisdom of creation has preceded the skill of industry. The skill used by artisans to set up their tents was designed based upon the example of the tree and its roots. It is obvious that this skill has been copied from the wisdom employed in propping up trees.

LEAVES

Consider the production of the leaves of the plants carefully. Within its texture and extending along its length and breadth is something comparable to the root system. Some of them have fine capillaries joined with thicker ones, all very stout and fine. If they were to be prepared by hand, man would not have been able to do the job on a single tree in a year's time. He would have needed implements, motion, design and instruction.

Within a few days time during the spring season, such abundant foliage comes into being that the mountains and lowland regions of the earth are filled without a word being spoken or a movement being made. You should know what the principle is that underlies these fine capillaries. They are interwoven in the texture of the leaves to irrigate them, just as the network of the capillaries in the body carries nutriment to all parts.

There is yet another wisdom in the thick veins of the leaves. Because of their resilience and strength, they keep the leaf from being torn. These leaves are similar to the artificial foliage manufactured from cloth and which are supported lengthwise and breadth wise and held fast against crumbling. As such the artificial manufacturing by hand follows the natural, though it can never reproduce the true spirit.

SEEDS

Consider the seed-stone embedded inside the fruit. It serves as a substitute in case a tree perishes due to some calamity. The same way one preserves those commodities that one is in constant need of at different places in order to preserve them in case one is lost or damaged. Also because of the seed's resilience and hardness, it keeps the fruit from getting too soft and succulent. If not for these seed-stone, the fruits would have split up and given way to instability.

Some seeds are edible while oil can be extracted from others. Now that you are aware of the purpose of the seed, you should consider the pulp that is within the date seed. Also ponder upon the benefits of the grape stone that produces that which is inedible such as the cypress and the poplar trees. Surely it is so that man may take enjoyment from them.

Consider the other benefits of plants. You will notice that they are affected by the autumn season, so that their vital heat gets enshrined in their twigs, and material for fruit production is engineered. The spring season clothes them with leaves and you get all kinds of fruit, just as you arrange different kinds of delicacies before you which have been cooked. Just behold the twigs presenting their fruit to you with their own hands.

And you gloat on the flowers which appear before you on their twigs as if they present themselves to you? Who has planned all this? Surely He Who Is the All Knowing Ordainer. And what purpose is served thereby? Surely, that man may enjoy the fruits and flowers. How strange, that instead of gratefulness for such blessings, men would deny the Donor altogether.

POMEGRANATE

Just consider the pomegranate and the skill and wisdom that has gone into its production. You will notice, inside it is all round and elaborate with grains laid layer upon layer, as if arranged by hand. The grains are divided into different parts and each part is wrapped up in a strap, fabricated in a uniquely exquisite manner. All these are enclosed in an outer rind.

The artistic ingenuity therein is that since the grains cannot help each other's growth of pulp, a membrane has been provided inside the pomegranate as a nutritive medium, in which are embedded both the grain and the pulp. These membranes help to keep them immovably fixed. Over all these, a stout covering is laid to keep them safe from external harm.

These are a few points concerning the pomegranate, to which anyone who wants a lengthy account, can add a lot more. The account given here is, however, sufficient for the purpose of argument and instruction.

CREEPER PLANTS

Just behold this weak creeper. These creepers bring forth such massive gourds, cucumbers and melons. What ingenuity has gone into its design! Since is was ordained that it will bear such large products, the plant is designed to spread on the earth. Had it been like other plants straight-standing, it would not have been able to bear its yield. It would have broken down before they ripened. See how it sprawls on the ground to put the burden of its products on the earth. You might have noticed that the roots of the gourd and the melon creepers spread in the earth with the products lying on the earth all round, just like a cat lying down lactating its young ones.

Consider the fact that these creepers grow only in set seasons suited to them in the fiery heat of summer, for example, when people welcome them joyfully. If they had flourished in winter, men would not like to bear their sight. In addition they may cause ailments in winter. It sometimes happens that cucumbers are produced in winter. The people avoid them generally, except the gluttons within a sense for harm and illness.

DATE PALM

Consider the date palms. There are female trees among them, for whose fertilization male plants are also generated. The males, like those animals, fertilize, but are themselves sterile.

Consider carefully the trunk of a date palm. You will find that it is woven like a web, though there are no long threads. It is as if a piece of cloth is woven with the hand to keep it stout and straight, capable of withstanding strong winds and of carrying massive bunches of fruit, on maturity, and then for roofing and bridging. You will find therein threads interwoven lengthwise and breadth wise. It is strong enough to be used in tool making. If it had been hard as stone, it could not have been used in buildings as wood, for example, doors, lattice work, wooden boards and boxes etc.

WOOD

There is one great benefit in wood. It floats on water. Everyone knows this but no one realizes its true worth. In the absence of this characteristic, how could boats have been built, which carry mountains of merchandise from city to city with much labour? What hardships would have had to be borne in transporting merchandise? Many articles of use would have disappeared from the market or would have been available only at great cost.

HERBS

Consider these herbs and the characteristics each has been endowed with as drugs. They penetrate down into the joints; eliminate waste products and toxic matters such as the Shahtra. Some others relieve hypochondria such as ateemoon. Some others remove flatulence such as vinegar. Some others absorb inflammation such as wild grapes.

Who then has endowed them with such properties? Surely He Who created them with a Purpose. Who gave men knowledge thereof? Surely He Who endowed these drugs with such properties. How could these matters have come to men's knowledge through mere chance and spontaneity, as the believers of chance claim?

Well, let us admit that man learnt all this through his intellect and reason, contemplation and experimentation. But who taught the animals? Some beasts, when they get injured, make use of herbs to get well, and some birds when suffering from constipation get well by purgation with sea water and so on?

You may, perhaps, doubt the utility of plant life and of the waste lands and plains, where no human life exists, and think it to be altogether meaningless and useless. It is not so. The wild animals feed thereon and their grain is used by the birds as food. Their twigs and wood is used as fuel by men.

There are other points as well which are worth noting. They serve as medicinal drugs. Hides are tanned. Cloth is dyed and so on. They possess limitless benefits.

WORTHLESS THINGS

Don't you know that the most lowly and despised plant is the Khairya Baradi? However, they too, possess various benefits. Paper is manufactured from it for use by the kings and populace. They are manufactured into mats for use by all. They are used in making lids to cover utensils made of glass etc., which are stuffed with them to prevent breakage. They have many other benefits in addition to these.

Then learn a lesson from the various benefits which are derived from beings small and big, and also from those things which have no worth and those that are valuable. The most worthless of all these are the cow dung and excreta. They are worthless pollution, but consider the benefits which arise from them for the agriculture and vegetables. The benefits are unparalleled. No vegetable can be worthwhile unless it is provided with manure which is so obnoxious that one abhors going near it.

Know this too, that the worth of a commodity does not depend upon its monetary value alone. It possesses two different values in two different markets. It sometimes happens that a commodity is worthless in the economic market and yet the same is valuable in the market of knowledge.

It may be that you consider a thing as worthless because of its low monetary value. However notice of what high value human excreta would have been had its properties been known to the alchemist. It is a fact that certain experiments of alchemy cannot be conducted without human excreta."

It was now time for the afternoon prayers, and the Imam (asws) told me to come the next day, inshaAllah.

I returned quite happy because of the information I had obtained from Imam (asws). I thanked Allah (swt) for the valuable information I received. I spent the night in perfect peace.

Chapter Five

FOURTH SESSION

NATURAL DIASTERS

After the usual prayers and address of the Almighty Allah, the Imam (asws) said, "O Mufaddal! I have given you in detail the arguments and observations in regard to the exact planning and design as regards human beings, the animal and the vegetable kingdom. They should be sufficient for those who wish to learn.

I now give you a detailed account of the calamities and catastrophes which occur at times and which these ignorant people marshal as argument for their denial of creation and purposeful Design of the Creator.

I shall also give in detail, the rationale of the troubles and miseries which the atheistic and Manichean Sect deny and shall also make mention of death and destruction which these sects have called into question, and what the naturalists of old have said.

Let this account serve as a refutation for those who argue that the universe came into being by sheer chance. May Allah (swt) destroy them - how they are being led astray. Some ignorant people have construed these events which occur from time to time, for example epidemics, jaundice, the absence of chlorophyll of the trees, hail storms, locusts, as an argument for the denial of Purposeful creation of the Creator.

The answer to this is that if there is no Designer of the universe, why is there not more severe catastrophes, as for example the complete disorder in the universe, the tearing apart of the earth, the cessation of sunrise, the drying up of river beds so as not one drop of water is left to moisten the lips, the air becoming stationary leading to the disorganization of all matter, the oceanic water submerging the earth? Who guards against all of these events? Whose planning is behind the scenes?

When you say if there had been a Designer and Creator, such swarms of locusts would not have visited us to cause such heavy damage, such virulent epidemics would not have taken millions of lives or hail storms would not have been so severe as to destroy our corn fields. If all these are real facts, why does not this universe get disorganized leading to the destruction of the whole world? Why does not the ocean submerge the earth with gushing water? Why does not the air become stationary to stifle all living beings? Why does not all this occur?

This shows that the Designer is there, Who prevents such occurrences in order that the universe may not become disorganized, the species become extinct, or that total annihilation takes place. What takes place is by way of the natural consequences of man's action, a warning and a preventive taking place now and then in the form of epidemics, locusts, ravages of crops and gardens, hail storms etc. This is a negation of the argument against purposeful creation. I ask of them why these epidemics and locust swarms do not continue forever so as to destroy the universe? They visit occasionally, and after a time, they leave.

Do you not see that this world is protected against these

horrible calamities and catastrophes? If any of these events occurred in this world, it would be completely annihilated. These calamities befall occasionally, in diluted severity, just to warn men to improve their conduct. They do not remain forever but get removed as and when men get dismayed in regard to their safety. These calamities befall as warning; and they get removed through Divine Grace.

TROUBLE FREE LIFE

The Manichean Sect has questioned the suitability of these calamities and troubles which befall men. Likewise, the atheists have failed to realise their true nature and dubbed them as meaningless. Both say that if this universe were governed by a Compassionate and Merciful Creator, these obnoxious occurrences would not have taken place. Those who use this argument try to conclude that if there had been a Creator then man's life would have been trouble free.

Had it been so, man's conceit and selfishness would have led him to the conduct which would not have been in accordance with religion or his religious life. Just as you find persons nurtured in luxury and comfort who mostly forget their manners and their state of having been brought up by somebody. They forget that they can receive some injury or sorrow or that some calamity may befall them. They even forget how to sympathise with some weak person or how to pity some needy person. They are not compassionate towards the feelings of others and do not show kindness to those with troubled souls.

However, when trouble befalls them, they feel its

veracity and are then open to reason. They are awakened to their ignorance and folly. They begin to act in a way which was incumbent on them all along. If this trouble had not befallen them, the would have continued to look upon themselves as gods, to spend their lives in conceit, to have no pity or sympathy with anybody else. Would such conduct have been in the interests of their religion and this world?

Certainly not! Along with defective religion, they would have suffered worldly harm. People would have hated them and condemned them. Such selfish persons would have created disorder in this universe in all affairs, industry, commerce, knowledge and mutual conduct etc. People who deny these matters, looking upon them as meaningless, are like those children who condemn bitter and distasteful medicine and get offended at the precautions against harmful foods. They dislike work, and like only to play freely, indulge in absurdities, to eat and drink without limit or hindrance. They do not know that such license and idleness would deteriorate their mental, moral and physical growth, that these delectable but harmful edibles would lead to different ailments and diseases. Their betterment lies in acquiring knowledge, and medicines hold many benefits for them despite a little unpleasantness.

They say as to why men have not been given sinless conduct so that the Almighty Allah may not have needed to chastise them with troubles. The answer to that is in such circumstances man would not have been worthy of any credit for goodness nor entitled to any reward.

If they then say, "What is the harm in having a life of

pleasure and comfort if he will not gain any credit or reward by virtue of his goodness", the answer will be to tell any rational and healthy person to sit idly whilst giving him assurances of the fulfillment of his needs without any efforts, then see if his mind agrees to it.

You will find him far better pleased and satisfied with the little he gets by his own effort rather than a great lot which comes to him unearned, without effort. Similarly the blessings of the Hereafter will be pleasing to them only when they are earned through effort.

Man is therefore allowed a two-fold blessing. Firstly, he gets a great reward for his effort in this world. Secondly, he has been shown the way to seek it by his own effort so as to get the maximum satisfaction for achievement. It is quite natural for a man to give no value to that which is obtained without effort or strife. However, he places great value on those things which he obtains through great effort and strife. As such, the blessings of the Almighty Allah which will be bestowed on him by virtue of his self-control within prescribed limits will be far more worthwhile to him in comparison, with a state of mind where he did not have to control his lusts and every unlawful thing had ceased to have any attraction for him. In that case, the blessings of the Hereafter allowed by the Almighty Allah would not have been so precious to him. The reward that he will get as a result of his intense effort and earning will be very much valuable to him.

If they then reply, "Does it not happen that some people are very pleased to get a blessing without any effort, then what argument is given for the people who feel gratitude for the blessings of the hereafter?"

The answer to them is if people become convinced, that they will get the blessings of the Hereafter without effort, then it will lead to all sorts of mischief, sinfulness and moral degradation and turpitude. Who would then have held himself back from moral turpitude or put in efforts is for virtuous conduct when he had known himself as a sure recipient of the blessings of the hereafter? Who could have been sure of the stage of life, honour and property of himself and of his family about the harm people would do in case there was no fear of punishment and retribution? The damage that would have been caused in this very life to the people before the Day of Judgment.

Justice and wisdom would have both been abandoned. It would have been questionable, if such irregularity and disorder had entered the Design. They also speak of the troubles and inconveniences which sometimes have a general application affecting the righteous and leaving the mischievous unharmed. They say, how can it be an appropriated design of the All Knowing, how do you explain such occurrences?

The answer to this will be that such troubles do befall the righteous and the mischievous all, and there are benefits for both categories ordained by the Almighty Allah. The righteous suffer troubles and inconveniences and a restitution of the blessings to them causes gratitude and perseverance in them. As for the mischievous, their trouble breaks from evil conduct.

There is a benefit of the betterment for all those who are spared from the impact of these troubles. Besides these two categories, for the righteous the state of goodness is a source of happiness and a further inducement and discernment for still better conduct. For the evil-doers also, the protection against harm is a special blessing from the Almighty Allah's Grace shown to them without them deserving it. This induces them to act kindly and to forgive those who do them harm. A critic may say that such troubles befall their properties, yet sometimes their physical bodies suffer even to destruction, like being burnt, being drowned, being carried away' by floods or being buried alive.

The answer to them will be that the Almighty Allah has ordained therein the good of both categories. For the virtuous because of the departure from this world and its troubles and miseries, and for the mischievous in that their capacity to sin is thereby cut off.

To sum up, the Almighty Allah diverts the consequences of all such actions by His All Knowing and All Powerful Authority towards betterment just as, when a tree is broken down by wind, a good carpenter turns it to beneficial uses.

Similarly, the Almighty Designer diverts the consequences of these calamities which befall their properties and their physical bodies to their benefit and betterment. If' someone asks as to why these calamities befall men, the answer will be, lest they become inclined to sinfulness. If there is a guarantee of safety, then the mischievous become completely indulged in sinfulness and the virtuous become lazy in doing good.

Both these modes of conduct over-power men when they are allowed a long lease of ease and comfort. Such occurrences keep them warned and deter them from such conduct—and therein lies their good. If they were altogether relieved of trouble, they would transgress the limits of sinfulness just as the people of bygone ages did, so that they had to be destroyed by deluges to clear the earth of them.

DEATH

There is one point fixed in the mind for these deniers of Design and Purpose, to wit, death and annihilation. They think that it would have been proper it men had been given everlasting lives without any trouble or harm.

It is necessary to carry the argument to its logical conclusion to see the consequences it leads to. Just see that if all men had lived everlasting lives. This earth would have become too narrow for them. They would not have had room enough for their dwellings, their agriculture and the provision of requirements for leading their lives. Notwithstanding the constant axe of death working all the time, while there are quarrels in regard to the dwellings and the cropping fields; even wars are fought with blood-shed on this account. What would have been their condition if no one had died while reproduction of new individuals continued? Now even when deaths continue, we have such difficulties.

What would have been the stakes if none had ever died? People would have been over-powered by greed, lust and hardheartedness. If they had been assured of everlasting lives, no one would have been contented with his possessions. No one would have liked to part with anything to the needy, nor would there have been any solace after a misfortune. They would have been tired of life and of all the mundane matters. The man with a long life gets tired of it and yearns for death to intervene and provide relief.

They said that it should have been so ordained that all troubles and ailments would have been removed from among them, so that they should not have longed for death nor should have been desirous of it. The reply to this is that they would have fallen into evil ways and disobedience.

If they say that to eliminate the difficulties due to shortage of housing and living conditions their reproduction could have been stopped, the reply will be that in that case untold numbers of creatures would have been denied entry into this world and thus deprived of the blessings of the Almighty Allah in this life and the Hereafter. In such circumstances, only one generation would have been allowed admittance without the capacity for further reproduction.

And then they may say that He (swt) should have created all men, those born and those to be born in the future, in one lot.

The answer to them will be, as stated already, that the contingency will arise as to the shortage of housing and husbanding facilities. Where could room enough have been found for houses to be built, agriculture to be carried on, communications to be established. In that case in the absence of sexual relationships, there would be no community interests among the kith and kin, no mutual help in times of hardship and distress. Whence would have been obtained the enjoyment of parentage in rearing up the offspring?

This shows clearly that regardless of the direction when one moves away from the Purposeful Design, it proves to be flawed, absurd and preposterous.

CRITICIZING THE DIVINE ORDINANCE

A criticizer may criticize the divine ordinance from another point of view and say: is there ordinance in this world while we see that powerful persons oppress, transgress and rape, the weak are wronged and humiliated, good people are poor and afflicted with distresses, bad people are sound and wealthy, sinners and criminals are not punished immediately? If there is in fact planned ordinance in the world, affairs should happen according to analogy: good people should be blessed, bad people should be deprived, powerful people should be unable to wrong the weak, and sinners should be punished immediately. It is said in answering this: if it were so, doing good, with which man has been preferred over other creatures, would disappear. People would not do good or benevolence expecting to be rewarded and trusting in what Allah has promised in return. People would be like animals that are led by whip and fodder. No one would act due to the certainty of being rewarded or punished until people would emerge from humanity into animality. What is not seen (the unseen) would not be known and no one would act except for the present pleasures of the worldly life. Even good people would act to earn livelihood and wealth in this worldly life only and those who refrain from oppression and sins would do that just for fear of immediate punishment until all people's deeds would be done only for the present and with no certainty of what is with Allah, and they would not deserve the reward of the hereafter or the eternal bliss in it; nevertheless, these things that the criticizer has mentioned —wealth and poverty, good health and affliction—are not contrary to his analogy, but they may happen according to that sometimes.

You may find many good persons who are granted with wealth for certain wisdom and lest people think that it is the atheists who are provided with the means of subsistence while the pious are underprivileged and thence prefer debauchery to piety. And you find that many transgressors are punished when their transgressions and harms increase against people and against themselves, as with Pharaoh when he was punished with drowning and Nebuchadnezzar was punished with getting lost and Belbis with killing. Allah may delay the punishment of some evildoers and postpone the reward of some good doers till the afterlife for some reasons unknown to people. This does not refute the planned ordinance. Many rulers in the earth do this without annulling their ordinances. In fact, their delaying of what they delay and hastening of what they hasten are considered within their right of statesmanship and farsightedness. Since all evidences and their analogy necessitate that things have a wise creator then what prevents this Creator from managing His creation? According to their analogy, a maker does not neglect his craft except for one of three reasons: inability, ignorance or evilness; but all of these are impossible in the creation of Allah the Almighty for an unable one cannot make such great, wonderful creatures, an ignorant one does not know what is right and wise, and an evil one does not try to create and establish such things. If it is so, then definitely the creator of these creatures manages them, although much of this management cannot be understood by people. The public does not understand much of the management of rulers nor do they know its reasons because they do not know the secrets of the rulers nor what is there in their minds. If the reason behind a certain management becomes known, it will be found as right and correct. If you have a doubt regarding some drug or food, and then it becomes clear to you in two ways or three that it is cold or hot, will you not judge that it is as you have found and then remove the doubt from your mind? So what about these ignorants?

Why do they not judge that this world has been created and managed by a Wise Creator, and deny that it has been created in spite of all the evidences before them that cannot be counted? If half of the world and what it contained were somehow ambiguous, whether correct or not, it would not be a good thinking or courtesy to judge that all the world had been established out of indifference and by chance because the other half would have accurate and perfect things that would refute such hasty, untrue opinions. How is it then that whenever one searches, he finds the utmost correctness and perfection so that nothing may come to one's mind unless it is found most right and perfect?

O Mufaddal, know that the name of the universe in Greek is "cosmos" which means embellishment. It has been called so by philosophers and wise people too. They called it so when they saw its perfect order and organization. They did not call it "order" or "organization" but called it "embellishment" to show that, besides its exactness and perfection, it was the utmost in beauty and splendor.

O Mufaddal! I wonder at those people who do not judge medicine to be faulty though they see doctors commit mistakes, but they judge the world to be neglected (with no manager) though they do not see anything neglected in it. I really wonder at the morals of those who claim to be wise but ignore morals among people and set their tongues free to abuse the Exalted Creator, glory be to Him! The wonder is at the wretched (Mani) when he pretends to have the knowledge of secrets while he is blind to the evidences of wisdom in the creation and claims that the creation is full of mistakes and the Creator is ignorant!

The oddest of all are the atheists who wanted to

perceive by the senses what could not be perceived by reason, and when they failed, they denied the existence of the Creator and said: why is He not perceived by reason? It is said: He is above the position of reason, as sight when does not see that which is above its position. When you see a stone rising in the air, you know that someone has thrown it. This knowledge comes not from the sight but out of reason, because it is reason that distinguishes and knows that a stone does not rise by itself. Do you not see how the eyesight stops at a point and does not exceed it? So does reason. It stops at a point in the cognizance of the Creator and does not exceed it, but it realizes His existence through reasoning. It is the same reason by which man realizes that there is a soul inside him though he does not see or feel it by any of the senses.

REASON AND THE CREATOR

And according to this too, we say: reason perceives the Creator in a way that necessitates man to acknowledge His existence, and it does not perceive Him in a way that necessitates man to know His qualities. If they ask: how is a weak man charged with knowing the Creator without knowing His qualities? It is said to them: people have been charged with what they can do and within their abilities, that is to believe in the Creator and to follow His orders and prohibitions, and they have not been charged with knowing His attributes. A king does not ask his subjects to know whether he is tall or short, white or brown; rather, he asks them to submit to his rule and follow his orders. Do you not think that if someone were to come to a king and say "present yourself to me so that I can know you fully;

otherwise, I will not follow your orders", he would expose himself to punishment? In the same way, he who refuses to believe in the Creator until he knows His essence will receive His wrath. And if they say: do we not describe Him when we say that He is the Mighty, the Wise, and the Generous? It is said to them: these are attributes of acknowledgment and not of description. We know that He is wise but we do not know the essence of His wisdom, and the same can be said about His other attributes. We see the heaven but we do not know its essence, and we look at the sea but we do not know where it ends. The examples of this cannot be counted, though they fail in comparison, but they lead the reason to know the Creator. If they ask: then why do people disagree over Him? It is said: because minds fail to recognize the extent of His greatness and exceed their capacities in searching to know Him, and they want to know everything about Him while they are unable to do that or even the least of it.

One of these examples is the sun that shines all over the world and yet no one knows its reality. There are too many sayings about it, and philosophers have disagreed over how to describe it. Some of them say that it is a hollow star full of fire with a mouth agitating with flames. Some others say it is a cloud. Some say it is a glass mass that concentrates heat and then sends rays. Some say it is a fine, clear mass of congealed seawater. Others say it is many parts of fires gathered together. Some others say it is a fifth element separate from the four elements. Then they have disagreed over its shape. Some of them say it is like a flat page. Others say it is like a ball. They have also disagreed on its size. Some say it is as big as the earth. Some others say it is less, and some say it is much greater than a great island. People of geometry say it is one hundred and seventy times bigger than the earth.

The disagreement in the sayings about the sun shows that people cannot realize its reality. Minds are unable to realize the reality of the sun, which eyes clearly see and senses easily feel, then how about what is beyond the senses and hidden from the minds? If they say: why is He hidden? It is said to them: He is not hidden with a means, as one who hides from people behind doors and walls. The meaning of our saying "He is hidden" is that He is invisible to the eyes and minds because He is beyond the extent of the faculties of eyes and minds, like the case with the sun which is a creation created by Him and cannot be realized by eyes and minds. If they say: why is He so greatly beyond that? This is a wrong saying because it does not befit One Who is the Creator of everything except to be different from everything and exalted over everything. Glory be to Him the Almighty.

If they say: how is it possible that He is different from everything and exalted over everything? It should be said to them that the truth about things can be known in four ways: first, to see whether that thing is existent or not; second, to know what it is in its essence; third, to know how it is and what its description is; and fourth, to know why and for what cause it is. There is nothing in this existence that man can know in the Creator as it is except that he knows that He exists. If we say: how and what is He? Knowing His essence and all things about Him is beyond the bounds of possibility. Or we say: for what is He? It is not valid in the description of the Creator because He, glory be to Him, is the cause of everything, and nothing is a cause for Him. The knowledge of man that He (the Creator) is existent does not necessitate that he know what and how He is, just as his knowledge that the soul is existent does not necessitate that he know what and how it is. The same can be said about other spiritual matters. If they say: now you describe Him due to the shortage of knowledge about Him as if He is unknown. It is said to them: it is so, on the one hand, if minds want to know His essence and description; and on the other hand, He is closer than every close one when His existence is proved by satisfactory evidences. From one side, He is clear to everyone, and from another side, He is so mysterious that no one can realize Him. So is reason. It is clear through its evidences whereas it is hidden in its essence.

The naturalists say that nature does nothing meaningless nor does it leave anything incomplete and claim that wisdom proves that. It is said to them: who has given nature this wisdom then, and how does it not exceed the limits of anything, which is something that minds fail to learn even after long experiments? If they prove wisdom and power to be of nature in doing such things, they will acknowledge what they have denied because these are the attributes of the Creator. But if they deny this to be of nature, then this is the creation calling out that it is the Wise Creator's.

From the ancient nations, there were some people who denied the divine will and management in things and claimed that things came into existence by accident and by chance. They took some signs which were unlike the usual, such as when one was born with a finger less or more or when one was born disfigured, as evidence showing that things were not under will and management but by accidents as they happened.

Aristotle refuted that by saying: that which comes into being by accident and chance is something that comes one time due to certain factors in nature making something unusual and not like the natural matters that happen in one form continually and successively.

O' Mufaddal, you see the different species of animals following a regular pattern and having identical shapes. For instance, a human infant when born has two hands, two legs with five fingers or toes in each limb. But sometimes, as for one who is born unlike the usual, it is because of some reason in the womb or in the substance from which the infant grows, as it happens in some crafts when a skillful craftsman wants to be accurate in his craft but some defect in the raw material or tools affects his production. Such a thing may happen to the children of animals for the reasons we have mentioned that a child may be born with less or more or disfigured limbs, but most of them are born sound with no defect.

The defects that happen in some things because of some shortage do not mean that all the things have come by accident with no maker. So are things in nature. The saying that things have come into existence by accident and chance is totally wrong and nonsensical.

If they say: why does such a thing happen? It is said to them: to know that things are not created inevitably by nature nor by something else, as some people say, but are created with will and management by a Wise Creator Who has made nature run most of the time in certain routines and sometimes in variation because of some temporary causes, so it is concluded that nature is managed by the Creator and it needs His power to attain its purposes and complete its acts. Blessed be Allah, the Best of creators.

O' Mufaddal! Take what (the knowledge) I have given you, and keep what I have presented you, and be to your Lord grateful, and to His blessings a praiser, and to His guardians an obeyer.

I have explained to you a part from the whole and a little from plenty of evidences of creation and proofs of the right management and ordinance. Think of them deeply and take a lesson.'

Mufaddal said, 'My master, with your assistance I acknowledge that and will inform of it Inshallah.' He put his hand on my chest and said, 'Keep (memorize) it by the will of Allah and do not forget, Inshallah.' I fainted to the ground, and when I regained consciousness, he said to me, 'How do you see yourself, Mufaddal?' I said, 'By the help and assistance of my master (Imam as-Sadiq asws), I am not in need of the book that I have written and the knowledge is before me as if I am reading it from my palm. Praise and thanks be to my master as he deserves.'

Imam (asws) said, 'O Mufaddal, make your heart attentive and prepare your attention, mind and tranquility for I shall deliver to you from the knowledge of the heavens and the earth and what Allah has created in them and between them of His wonderful creatures, and all kinds of angels and their ranks and positions up until the farthest lote-tree, and of the rest of the creation from the jinn and human beings to the lowest seventh earth and what there is under the soil so that what you perceive shall be a part of many parts. You may leave if you want with the mercy and blessings of Allah. You are to us in an honorable place, and your position in the hearts of the believers is as the position of water to the thirsty. Do not ask me about what I have promised you until I myself tell you.'

Mufaddal said, 'I left my master with that which no one had ever left with.'"

ABOUT WILAYAT MISSION

As followers of Masoomeen (asws), we have been ordered by Allah to spread His commands to those "who were not present". If one hears of the command of Allah and does not convey it to others, then no excuse will be accepted from him and he will be thrown into hell. It is wajib upon all to convey the message of wilayat e Ali (asws) as this is the command of Allah. However there are so few books of hadiths and sayings of Masoomeen (asws) that have been translated that it makes it very difficult for momineen to share the words of Masoomeen (asws) with others. We hope that our mission will not only make it easy for momineen to fulfill their duties and obey the command of Allah to spread wilayat e Ali (asws), but that we will have also fulfilled our obligation in spreading this command of Allah and gained the pleasure of Masoomeen (asws) instead of Their anger.

We pray that not only will our iman and marifat be increased but that of every person as well. We pray to our Imam (atfs) to help us and guide us so that we do not go astray and do not lose sight of our true mission which is;

SPREADING THE TRUE RELIGION OF ALLAH, WILAYAT E ALI (ASWS)

www.WilayatMission.org

www.ingramcontent.com/pod-product-compliance
Lightning Source LLC
Chambersburg PA
CBHW061327040426
42444CB00011B/2802